Computing Texts

A web notebook

A first course in using the
Internet and web design

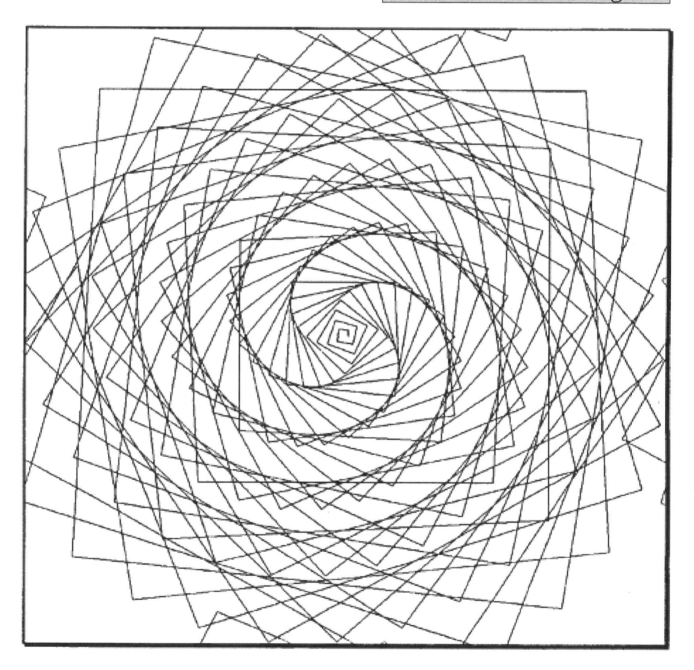

Tony Hawken

ISBN: 978-1-4457-2424-9

Preface

Aim

The aim of this book is to provide a structured course for those studying on an Access to Higher Education programme where Computing is one of the main options chosen. More specifically it is for an introductory Internet computing course where the Internet, World Wide Web, and Web Design using HTML is to be studied.

Although intended for an Access to Computing course, it will also be of use to other students. If you were to study for a BTEC National in IT, it is very likely that you will have to study a number of units that involve Web Design and the management of web sites. It is highly likely that if you study Computer Science in a foundation year, you will also have to learn much of what is contained in this book.

Origins

Quite a number of years ago, I started teaching computing on an Access to Higher Education course. The computing part of the course consisted of six units – 3 on C++ programming, one unit on using the Internet and two that involve creating web pages with HTML. The 3 units that appear in this book correspond to the last three mentioned. These units were, and continue to be validated by OCN. More specifically they are:

1. Using the Internet (CDO/2/LN/127)   - level 2 unit
2. Web site development – HTML (CK8/3/LN/002) – level 3 unit
3. Further web site development (CK8/3/LN/003) – level 3 unit

The first of these units started off as a level 3 unit, but was thought to be too simple for that level, and so was down-graded. I have added much material that I feel would be appropriate to teach. If OCN were to take these ideas on board this could once again be a level 3 unit.

I have also added material to the other two modules. In particular I feel that there should be much more emphasis on CSS and style sheets. The CSS box model is not even mentioned in any of the units for HTML and web design. I feel that this should be incorporated into some of their course units.

Approach

The material in this book is designed to be informal and easy to use. It is a very practical "How to do" book, where the emphasis is trying things out. There is very little theory – just enough, in my opinion to make sense. The bulk of the book is made up of simple examples with brief notes to explain how things work. In the case of the two units that deal with web design, there are a number of example html documents, or style sheets, screen dumps to show you what to expect, and some notes commenting on the code.

There are 3 parts to this book. Each part corresponds to a module taught on the Access to Computing course. These parts are divided up into 5 chapters or weeks. Each chapter should take a week to complete. This involves 3 hours of teaching per week in college, and between 2 and 3 hours homework per week. The 3 hours teaching per week at college should involve about 40% practical work, this could mean searching the Internet, or in later units creating web pages etc.

There is possibly too much material in the book. This is intentional, as it provides more scope for the more able student. Any teacher who adopts this book for use in a class should be aware of this. It is possible that they will choose to omit sections. The extra material will allow for differentiated teaching.

Resources

If you are using a PC that runs a fairly recent version of the Windows operating system, you will already have most of the software required to follow the course in this book. To access web pages on the Internet you need to have a web browser. You will probably have Microsoft Internet Explorer if you are using Windows. Other browsers such as Mozilla Firefox can be downloaded from the Internet.

I have made a conscious decision to develop web pages using a text editor such as notebook. Firstly, you will already have a copy. Secondly, you will be forced to write all the HTML yourself. The alternative would be to use an HTML editor, or a WYSIWIG web development package. Adobe Dreamweaver is far too expensive, and Microsoft FrontPage, although much cheaper, does not do a particularly good job. Writing your own HTML is a very useful skill. Whatever software professional developers may use, all of them will be able to code HTML using an editor.

Besides the software already mentioned, you will need to have access to software to produce a report for your assignment. Most people will have access to a version of Microsoft WORD. If you don't you can download OpenOffice from the Internet. This is an integrated package, similar to Microsoft Office, with the added bonus that it looks similar and is compatible with Microsoft Office. Even if you have Microsoft Office, I would recommend downloading the most recent version of OpenOffice, as there are some things that it does better than Microsoft Office.

To provide evidence that your web page looks like it should, you will need to be able to provide a screen dump. This is achieved by pressing on the Print screen key. I then paste the image into Microsoft Paint, so that I can crop the image before saving it.

Final word

This book makes no pretences at being complete, and in many cases may be too brief. For that reason, it is recommended that other books are consulted – see the bibliography for suggestions.

Contents

Part 1

Using the Internet and Email

Aims

After completing this 5-week unit, you will be able to do the following:

Web browsers and Internet search

Be able to use main facilities of a web browser to navigate web pages on the Internet.

Download, save and print both web pages and pictures within a web page.

Perform advance search with Boolean operators.

Email

Be able to use the main facilities of an email program such as Microsoft Outlook Express.

Be able to add contacts and groups of contacts to an address book for later use.

Be able to set up and use web-mail.

Basic security

Be able to use the main features of a security suite such as AVG Internet security.

Be able to change browser settings to improve the security of your computer.

Internet Protocols and how the Internet works

Be able to appreciate the main Internet protocols, and understand what they do.

Understand how web pages are downloaded, and how email works.

Be able to use commands associated with the Internet protocols such as FTP, and also other Internet utilities.

Chapter 1 (week 1)

Internet search using a browser

1.1   Key concepts

The Internet

The Internet is a huge collection (many thousands) of computer networks connected by means of various communications technologies. Within each network there will be one, or possibly many computers.

A simple home computer is likely to have a modem, or these days if you have broadband with a number of computers in the house, a wireless router with a built-in modem, that enables you to connect to the Internet via an **internet service provider** (ISP). An **ISP** is merely someone you pay to provide you with an Internet service, much in the same way that you pay a telecommunications company such as BT for the use of a telephone service. The physical connection that enables you to receive data from the Internet, is usually the phone line, which also allows you to make telephone calls. For this reason your ISP and telephone service provider, are often the same company.

The world-wide-web (WWW)

The World-Wide-Web (WWW) was conceived by Tim Berners-Lee in 1990 at CERN as a means to publish information and make it available on the Internet.

The World-Wide-Web can be thought of a huge collection of documents or web pages stored on very many (millions of) computers throughout the Internet. Each computer that stores these documents will have on them one or more web-sites made up of one or more web pages.

The web pages are written using a mark up language called HTML. They will appear as files with the extension .htm or .html. Within these files you have text that you wish to be read, instructions that format the text in a particular way, pictures and links to other web pages called hyperlinks.

Hypertext Mark-up Language (HTML)

HTML is a simple language, which is mainly used to format text. It has many similarities to a text formatting language called **nroff**, which was commonly used on all **unix** systems in the seventies and eighties. The nroff program predates word-processors, and was used to format text files to produce something that looks like a word-processed document. Unlike nroff that formats documents for a printer, HTML is used to format documents to be viewed on a screen.

HTML gets its name from another feature that is important in all HTML documents – hypertext or the use of hyperlinks.

Hyperlinks are pointers in the text document, which either allow you to move to a different part of the same document, or to move to a completely different document. They can points to documents on the same computer or network, or to a document on a computer halfway across the world.

HTML documents can also include pictures, video and sound files.

Browsers

A browser is a program that can read the contents of a file, but is unable to modify the contents. Browsers usually have the facility to move to different parts of the document stored in the file, and display a screen-full of the document at a time.

Text browsers

A text browser is a program that enables you to read text files, and be able to move about the text document and display one screen full of information at a time.

Web browsers

A web browser is a program which allows you to read HTML documents. The HTML documents can be on your computer, or on another computer - many miles away.

An HTML document is a text file that contains commands to format the text in the same manner that a word-processor formats text for you. That is you are able to have different fonts, different size fonts, underline, italics and many other features that you would expect from a word-processing program. A browser needs to be able interpret these commands and carry out the appropriate formatting.

The most popular web browsers in current use are:

1. Microsoft Internet Explorer

2. Mozilla Fircfox

Web browsers such as Internet Explorer are called web browsers, as they are normally used to view documents on the world-wide-web (Internet). They can also be used to browse any HTML document that you have on your computer, as well as any text file that you have available.

If the HTML document which you wish to view is on the internet, on someone else's computer, and you are currently logged onto the internet, the first thing the browser has to do is load the document to you computer. This simply means that the document file you want is copied from another computer to your computer via the Internet. This document is stored in a piece of temporary storage on you hard-disk called a **cache**.

It is now an easy matter for the web browser to display the text in the document, and provide appropriate formatting according to the HTML commands present in the document.

If, while reading your HTML document, you click on a **hyperlink**, then the document linked by this hyperlink will be the next one to be read. If this document is not available on your computer, the browser will have to load the document via the Internet onto your computer, before you can read it.

1.2   Using a web-browser (Mozilla Firefox)

Clicking on an icon for Mozilla Firefox will enable you to load the browser.

It is assumed that you will want to use the browser to access documents on the Internet. This is referred as being **online**. These days most people have broadband internet, so clicking on the icon will also load your homepage.

The following screen is typical after first logging on to the Internet using Mozilla Firefox. In this case I have configured my Internet settings, so that the homepage is set to http://www.google.co.uk/

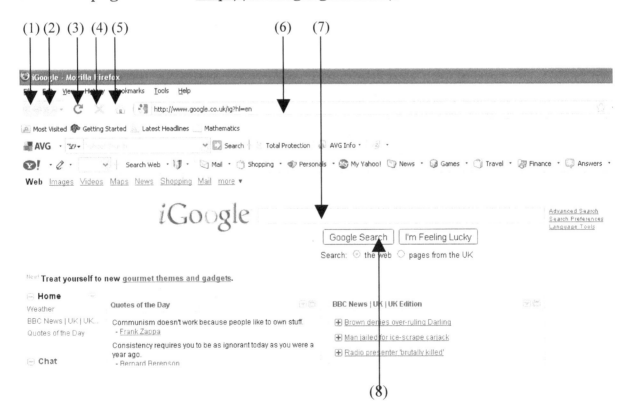

The browser contains a variety of buttons and pop-down menus that make accessing the Internet very easy to do. In particular you need to be familiar with the following:

1. Go back to previous document

2. Go forward to next document

3. Refresh the web page

4. Stop. Press this to stop searching.

5. Home. This is the first page loaded when you click on the Mozilla Firefox icon.

6. Address bar - contains current URL

The following are part of the Google web page.

7. Search bar. Queries are entered here.

8. Google search button. Click here once you have entered your query, otherwise press return.

Pop-down menus

The following pop-down menus form part of the Mozilla Firefox browser.

File   - any thing to do with files. Use for saving and printing HTML documents.

Edit   - typically used for cut and paste operations

View   - useful for stop, and refresh options

History   - records all the web sites that have been visited

Bookmarks - useful to save a useful URL (Internet Explorer refer to these as favourites)

Tools   - A variety of useful tools including security settings etc,

Help   - tells you how to use Mozilla Firefox

Tools pop-down menu

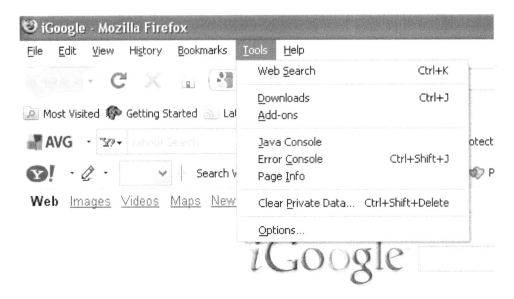

Options

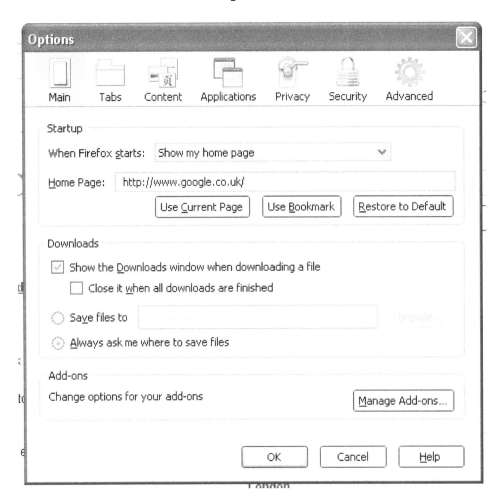

The main page of Options, is probably the most useful, as it allows you to change your homepage. You should also have a look at security and privacy. The advanced tab covers all the security and privacy settings.

1.3   Using a web-browser (Internet Explorer)

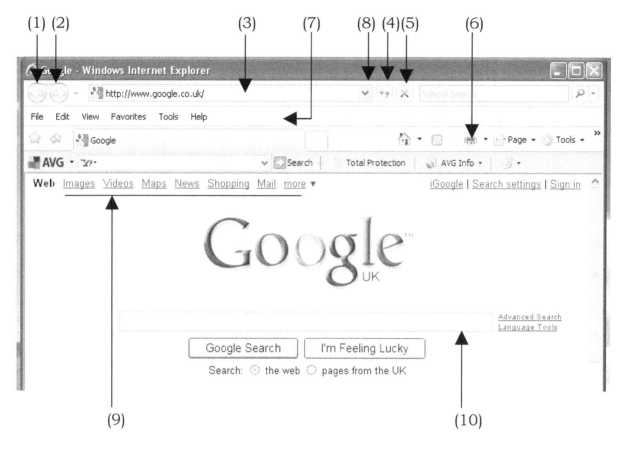

The browser contains a variety of buttons and pop-down menus that make accessing the Internet very easy to do. In particular you need to be familiar with the following:

1. Go back to previous document

2. Go forward to next document

3. Address bar - contains current URL

4. Refresh web page

5. Stop. Press this to stop searching.

6. Print page

7. Menu bar - can get pop-down menus by clicking on these.

8. Use this to retrieve previously entered URL's

The following are part of the Google search engine:

9. Hyperlinks - These are part of the document being read. You can click on these to read another document. Hyperlinks are often underlined.

10.   Search bar – type in your search here.

Pop-down menus

The following pop-down menus form part of the Internet Explorer browser.

File   - any thing to do with files. Use for saving and printing HTML documents.

Edit   - typically used for cut and paste operations

View   - useful for stop, and refresh options

Favourites - useful to save a useful URL (often referred to as bookmarks)

Tools   - A collection of tools, many of which are involved with security and internet access.

Go   - can use this to go to a different address, or a file on your computer.

Help   - tells you how to use Internet Explorer

Tools pop-down menu

Tools   Help
Delete Browsing History...
Pop-up Blocker ▶
Phishing Filter ▶
Manage Add-ons ▶
Subscribe to this Feed...
Feed Discovery ▶
Windows Update
Windows Messenger
Diagnose Connection Problems...
Spybot - Search & Destroy Configuration
Internet Options

More about these menus will be said later.

1.4   Entering an address

Every page on the web has a unique address. These are often referred to as **Uniform Resource Locators** (URL).

The following are examples of URLs:

1. http://www.mathcs.richmond.edu

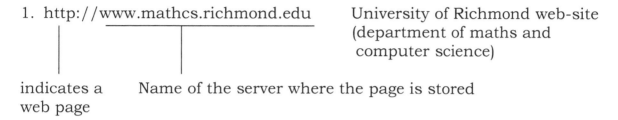

University of Richmond web-site (department of maths and computer science)

indicates a web page

Name of the server where the page is stored

2. www.mathcs.richmond.edu

   Unless you use a really ancient web-browser it is not necessary to enter http//:

3. www.mathcs.richmond.edu/~hubbard

Directory or folder

   Directory of person with the username hubbard (~username is a facility used on all unix systems to identify directories belonging to particular users etc).

4. www.mathcs.richmond.edu/~hubbard/Books.htm

   The file Books.htm is to be found in the top-level directory of the user with username hubbard.

As you can see from the previous examples, A URL can be used to identify:

- The address of a web-server
- A directory on a particular web-server.
- A file within a particular directory, on a given web-server.

URL's or addresses can be entered in the address bar of Internet Explorer Or Mozilla Firefox (or whatever your browser is). If you then press return or double click the address with your mouse, the given web page will be loaded on to your computer.

1.5 Download, save and print web pages and pictures

You download a web page every time you go onto the Internet. To download a page means that a copy of the web page is copied onto the hard-drive of your computer. This has to happen before it can be displayed on the screen.

1.5.1 Saving pages using Mozilla Firefox

The following web page was downloaded by entering its URL. A copy of the corresponding HTML file and associated images are stored on the hard drive. You can save the entire web page and images using the **Save Page As ...** option.

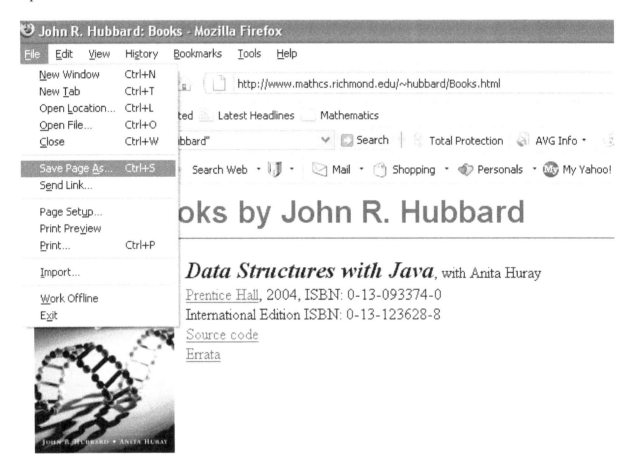

There are a number of formats that you can save a web page. Usually you will want to do one of the following if you are using Mozilla Firefox.

1. Web page complete stores the web page and associated pictures. These pictures will be saved in a new folder.

2. Web Page, HTML only will save the html file only.

You will also need to be able to specify where you want to save the web page. This can be done by clicking on (1) amd choosing the drive and folder where you want to store the files.

You can choose the file format to save the web page (2), and what you want to call it (3)

Options for saving a web page (Mozilla Firefox)

(1)

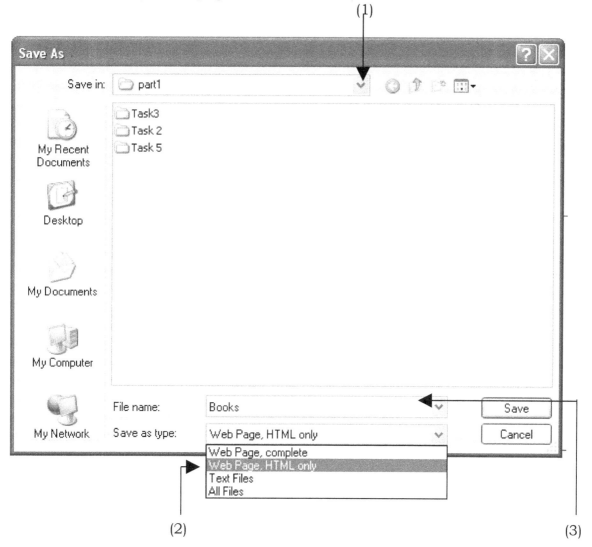

(2)   (3)

The following screen dump shows the html file and associated folder for storing the pictures.

You will notice that the html file has an icon associated with Internet Explorer, even though the browser being used was Mozilla Firefox. This is because in this instance the default browser was set as Microsoft Internet Explorer.

1.5.2   Saving web pages using Microsoft Internet Explorer

If you use Microsoft Internet Explorer as you browser to obtain this web page, how you can save the web page is slightly different. The **Save As ...** option is equivalent to the **Save Page As ...** option using Mozilla Firefox. Also there are more options for formats to save the web page.

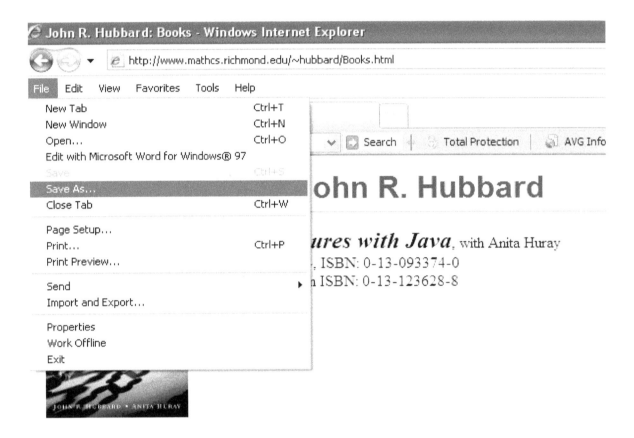

Options for saving a web page (Microsoft Internet Explorer)

You will notice that there are 3 options that you will consider when saving your web page.

1. Webpage complete - will save the html file and the pictures in a separate folder.

2. Web Archive, single file – will save the html file and all the pictures into a single file with file extension .mht.

3. Webpage, HTML only – will save just the html file.

Options for saving a web page (Microsoft Internet explorer)

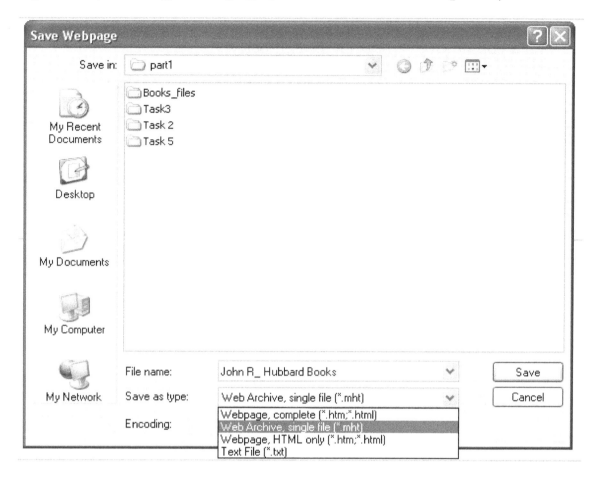

The following screen dump shows the MHTML file that contains the web page and pictures.

1.5.3   Printing web pages

Mozilla Firefox and Microsoft Internet Explorer have the same facilities for printing web pages. From the File pop-down menu, you have the following options:

Print preview   -   Display what the page will look like as one or more
                                printed pages.

Print   -   Print the current web page

1.5.4   Saving pictures

The easiest way to save a picture is to right-click on the picture. You will then obtain a pop-down menu as illustrated below.

In the case of Mozilla Firefox you click on the option **Save Image as ...**

In the case of Microsoft Internet Explorer you click on the option **Save Picture As ...**

When you do this you can select a folder where you want the image file to be stored.

Mozilla Firefox   **Microsoft Internet Explorer**

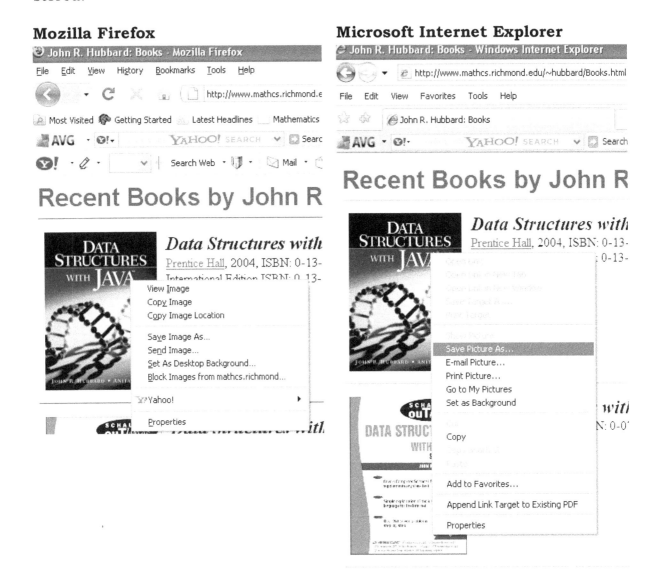

You will notice that both browsers have the option to copy the image. If you click on **Copy image** or **Copy**, depending on what browser you are using, you can copy the image into another document such as a WORD file by using a paste operation.

1.6   Using Favorites (bookmarks)

A favorite is a previously store link containing the URL of a web-site of interest.

The Favorites pop-down menu

The Favorites button is used to save a link to the URL of your current web-site. It can then be used to access the web-site by clicking on the previously stored link.

To save a favorite:

1. Click on the Favorites button

2. Click on Add to favorites

To access a previously visited web-site using these favorites:

1. Click on the Favorites button

2. Click on the required link (You will see an Internet Explorer icon for each link)

If you use Mozilla Firefox, the equivalent feature is called a bookmark. This also stores the URLs of web sites that you have saved.

To save a bookmark:

1. Click on the bookmark button

2. Click on Bookmark this Page

To access previously store bookmarks:

1. Click on the bookmark button

2. Click on the required link.

The Bookmarks pop-down menu

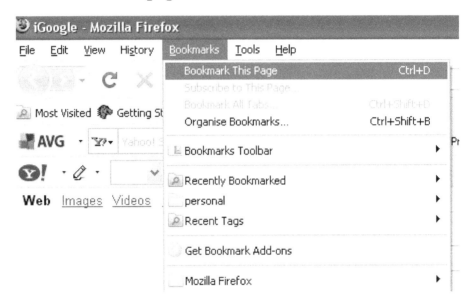

1.7   Examining your history

The history is a record of all the web sites that you visit. This can be a useful feature if you log out of you browser, or if your browser software crashes and you want to return to an interesting web page that you have not stored in your bookmarks (favorites).

Mozilla Firefox

It is easy to access your history when you use Mozilla Firefox. Just click on the **History** pop-down menu. This will give you a selection of the most recent sites visited.

To obtain a complete history since the history was cleared – click on **Show All History**. This option also displays the full URL visited.

Show all History

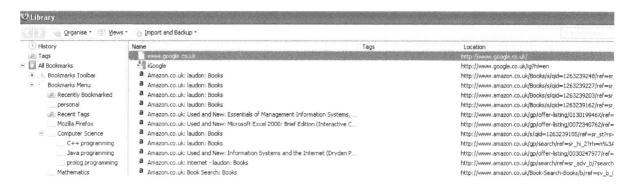

If you are using Microsoft Internet Explorer, it is not so obvious how to obtain your history of sites visited. Click on (1) to scroll down and show history. Then click on (2) to scroll down further. You will also note that it shows files that you have visited on your computer.

(1)

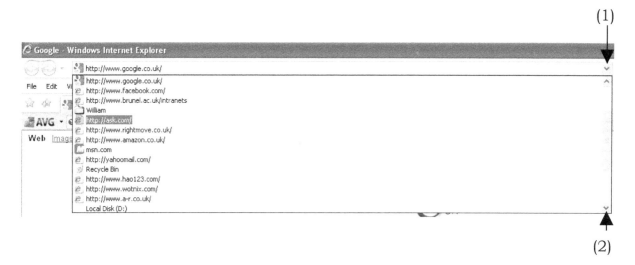

(2)

The other thing to note is, once you start typing in an address on the address bar, the addresses of those sites visited previously, will appear if they contain the characters that you have typed.

1.8 Changing the Internet options

What follows is an illustration on some changes that you can make to Microsoft Internet Explorer.

You can find the **Internet Options ...** In the **Tools** pop-down menu

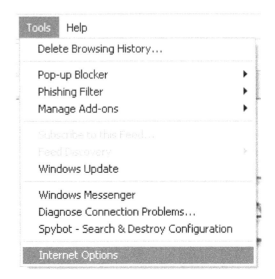

The only changes to the Internet options that we will consider at the moment can be found in the **General** section.

You can change your homepage by typing in the URL of the required site. Then click on **Apply**.

You can Delete cookies or delete temporary Internet files by clicking on the appropriate buttons. This is an aid to privacy.

You can also Clear the web history by clicking on the button **Clear History**.

The same sorts of changes can be made when you use Mozilla Firefox.

Options ... can be found in the **Tools** pop-down menu

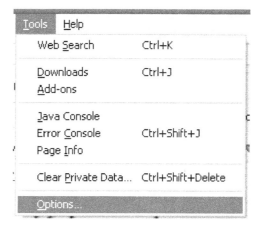

In the main tab for options, you can change your homepage. Simply type in a new URL for the homepage and then click on OK.

The other tabs you will need to look at are Privacy, Security and Advanced. Advanced contains information about privacy and security. You change the settings by clicking on radio buttons.

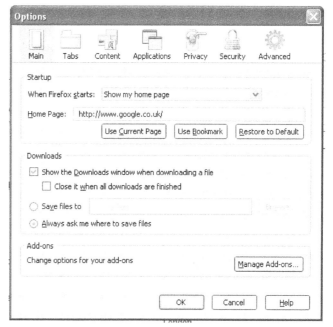

Exercise 1-1

1. **Download, save and print a web page and pictures**

   (a) Create a folder called Ex1-1

   (b) Enter the url:

   > http://www.mathcs.richmond.edu/~hubbard/Books.html

   (c) Save the complete web page including all images into the folder you created.

   (d) Save the picture corresponding to the book "Data structures in C++".

   (e) Click on the link errata for this book and save in the folder Ex1-1.

   (f) Click on the link source code to download the source code. Choose the option save As ... to save the file into the folder Ex1-1.

   (g) Obtain a print preview of this web page and record the number of pages if it were printed.

   (h) Bookmark this page, so that you can return to it later. If you are using Microsoft Internet explorer save it as a favorite.

2. **Internet Options**

   (a) Load Internet Explorer and click on the Tools pop-down menu. From this menu, click on Internet Options.

   (b) Click on the general Tab. Make sure that your homepage is set to www.google.co.uk. If it isn't, set it to this address.

   (c) Click on the programs tab. Check what program is being used as your HTML editor. If it is set to notepad, change it to the version of Microsoft Word or Open Office that you have installed.

   (d) Go to favorites and click on the link to the Hubbard books web page.

   (e) Edit this page using your HTML editor (Word or OpenOffice). Save the result in the folder Ex1-1

1.9 Search Engines

A search engine is a program that does the following:

- It allows you to enter a query which consists of a single keyword or short phrase
- It searches its database to try and match your query
- It displays a list of hyperlinks corresponding to the matches found in the database

Search engines collect and store information about numerous sites on the Internet. They automatically scan the web, following links from one site to another. As they do so they categorise the sites visit, storing the URL, and various keywords. From the information it collects, it is able to classify each web-site.

Search engines also keep their information up-to-date by looking out for new sites, and also updating existing ones in their database. In many respects they are much more effective than web directories, as information on the web soon becomes out-of date. Web directories generally need to be updated manually.

The following are examples of popular search engines:

1. www.altavista.com

   Altavista is a comprehensive and powerful search engine. It was developed in 1995 by the Digital Equipment Corporation. It has been awarded more search-related patents than any other company in the world.

2. www.yahoo.com or (www.yahoo.co.uk)

Provides both a web directory and search engine. This was one of the first search sites on the Internet and is still very popular for general searches. Yahoo is also one of the most comprehensive web-directories; it is much more suited to browsing and general search.

3. www.google.com or (www.google.co.uk)

Provides comprehensive search facilities - with a rating system based on other sites. Google now has the largest database of sites to search – in excess of 4 billion web pages. It also has a web-directory created by the Open Directory Project.

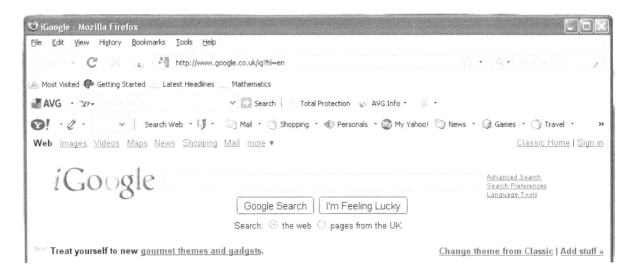

4. Excite

Excite is a popular Internet Portal that provides powerful search facilities. As well as providing the expected Boolean operators, it also provides parentheses for creating more complex queries

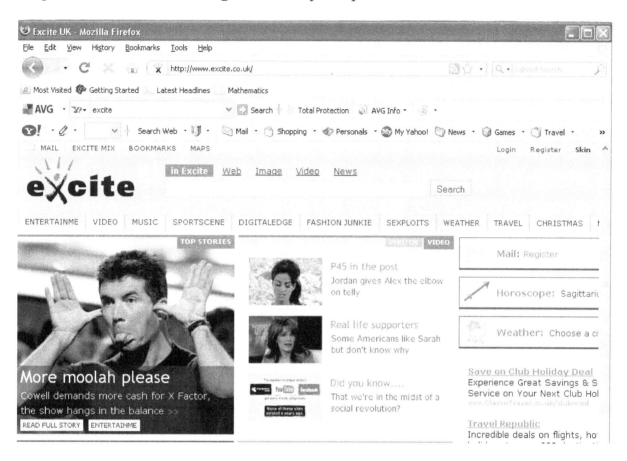

5. Ask Jeeves

Ask Jeeves is primarily used for searching using natural language queries. However Boolean operators can also be used. An advanced query facility is also available.

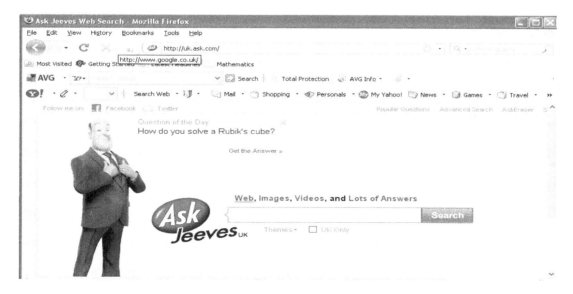

Many commercial sites provide their own directories and search engines to access their products. A good example of this can be found at **www.amazon.co.uk** or (**www.amazon.com**). This is a very useful site to compare the price of books, and also read reviews about various books. You can sometimes save as much as 40-50% of the price of a book by ordering online.

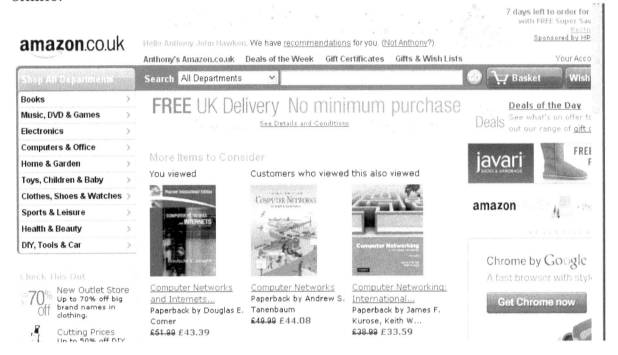

Obtained by clicking on Books, then Advanced Search

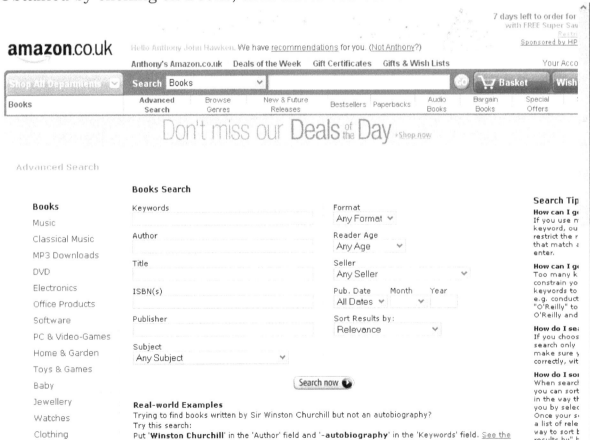

1.10   Entering queries in google

Results generated by the google search engine for the query - A level Chemistry. Nowadays, you also get prompted for suggestions whenever you enter a query in the search box.

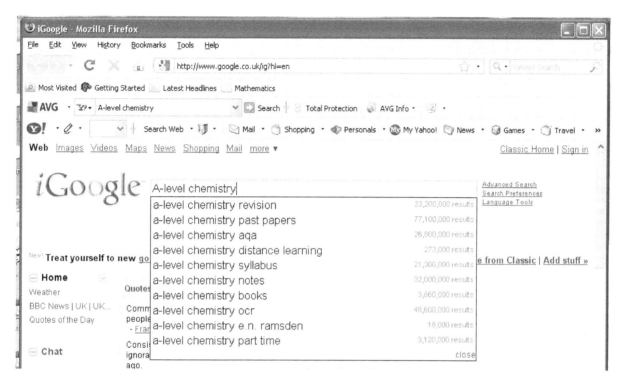

If you press return, you get a window like this. Typically there are 10 links per page, and they are sorted by relevance.

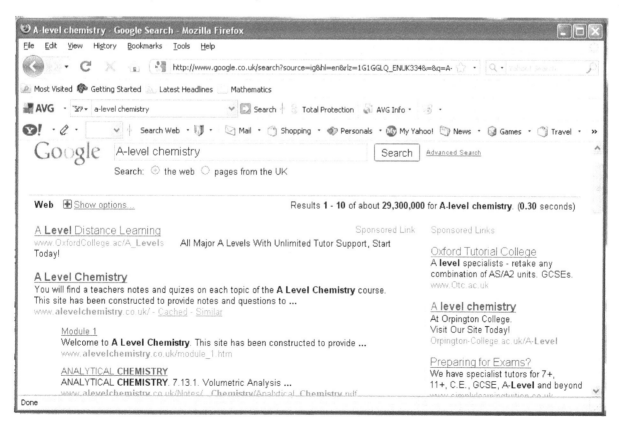

Notes :

1. The query entered above was - A level Chemistry

2. The above query is equivalent to A + level + Chemistry

3. This generated far too many results - most of them are not relevant (29,300,000). You can also take the figure shown as being far too high.

4. A better query would have been - "A level Chemistry"

5. The use of quotes indicates that the sequence of keywords are to be taken literally. That is it will only look for sites that have these words in the correct order.

6. You can also restrict the number of links, by clicking on pages from the UK – assuming that you only want information from the UK.

1.11   Advanced search

This section adds a little more detail about formulating queries for search engines.

The most basic type of query is a pattern-matching query. This is merely a keyword or group of keywords. The search engine will then search its database for all web pages where there is a match and will then return a URL corresponding to each match. Under what conditions you get a match, is determined by the search engine being used.

The following are typical criteria used by different search engines:

1. The keywords are to be found some where in the document.

2. The keywords are to be found in the first 100 words of the document.

3. The keywords are to be found in the title of the document.

In the above, it should be noted that the keywords do not have to appear together, and the order that they appear doesn't matter either. So you would expect to obtain very many hits formulating queries in this manner - many of them not being useful.

A more useful query would be one where you specify that the keywords have to appear together and in a certain order. This is achieved by placing the keywords between double quotes.

Boolean queries

Internet search engines typically allow you to use the Boolean operators to combine sub-queries. Boolean logic uses the following operators:

OR, AND, NOT

The meaning of these Boolean operators can be illustrated as follows:

A AND B   document contains both the words A and B

A OR B   document contains either A or B or both.

NOT A   The document doesn't contain the word A.

How to implement these queries varies depending on the search-engine being used. For that reason I will be giving you some examples, for the most popular search-engines.

1.12   Example queries for several search-engines

Google

Type of search	Example	Comment
Phrase search	"industrial revolution"	Search for words in the order given
AND search	Edison "light bulb" Edison + "light bulb"	Search for Edison and light bulb in any order.
OR Search	Edison OR "light bulb"	Search for word Edison or "light bulb".
NOT search	Edison -"light bulb"	Search for documents Edison but not "light bulb"

AltaVista

Type of search	Example	Comment
Phrase search	"Battle of trafalgar"	Search for words in the order given.
AND search	+London +"art museum"	Search for words London and "art museum"
OR search	Stratford Shakespeare	Search for the words Stratford or Shakespeare
NOT search	+python -monty	Search for documents with the word python that don't include monty.

Ask Jeeves

Type of search	Example	Comment
Phrase search	"Battle of trafalgar"	Search for words in given order
AND search	Asia Business	Search for words Asia or Business in any order.
OR search	Justice OR Judicial	Search for the words justice or Judicial
NOT search		Can't do this

Yahoo

Type of search	Example	Comment
Phrase search	"Battle of trafalgar"	Search for words in given order.
AND search	+Asia +Business	Search for words Asia and Business in any order.
OR search	Asia Business	Search for the words Asia or Business in any order.
NOT search	Asia -Business	Search for the words Asia but not Business

1.13   Search strategies

If for a given query there are too few hits, then you need to generalize your search. This can be achieved by:

1. Eliminate one or more highly specific keywords from the query.

2. If you use a Boolean query, remove one or more keywords and phrases that use the AND operator.

3. Try using keywords which are more general

4. Use a metasearch engine or directory instead.

If for a given query there are too many hits, then you need to specialize your search. This can be achieved by:

1. Add more keywords

2. If you use a Boolean query, include the AND operator and another keyword.

3. Just review the first 20 URL's. Search engines tend to put the best matches first.

4. If this fails use a directory instead.

1.14   Google Advanced Search page

The Google Advanced Search page can be obtained by clicking on the link "Advanced Search". This facility makes it very easy to present more complicated queries with very little knowledge about entering a query.

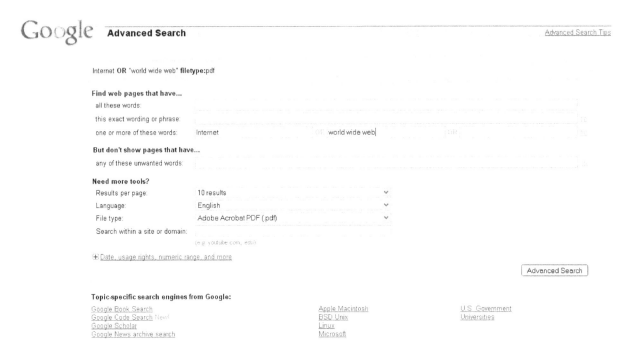

The above example is equivalent to the query:

Internet OR "world wide web" + filetype:pdf

However this query does not cover all of the attributes filled in. In particular if we were to enter a query instead of using The Advanced Search page, we are unable to specify the language or the number of results per page. So, there are some things that you specify with this page that you cannot do with a normal query.

I should also note that if you are familiar with this special syntax, there are some queries that you can do with an advanced query that you cannot do with this advanced search page. For instance, How would you specify that you want documents written in English or French.

The special syntax includes the following useful keywords:

intitle: words must appear in the title of webpages
intext: words must appear in the text of webpages
site: can specify a given top level domain to restrict the search
inurl: can restrict the search to a single url
daterange: can restrict search to documents created within a range of dates
filetype: specify a given filetype (eg. pdf, ppt, xls, doc etc.)

Exercise 1-2

1.8.1 Internet Search

(a) Using a search engine such as Google, enter the query "Janet and John". Record the number of hits and write down the URL of a useful links.

(b) If you know that your search is to do with the series of children's books called Janet and John, write to further queries that will refine your search. Record the number of hits and the URL of a useful link for each of your queries.

(c) Use the advanced search facilities within Google. Enter a query that will search for Janet and John books where the format of the files is pdf and the documents are based at an academic institution in the UK. i.e. the top-level domain is .ac.uk.

(d) Try repeating these tasks using a different search engine. Record your findings as before.

2. Searching for yourself

(a) Search for your name using a search engine such as Google. Record the number of hits. Also try and find a link that refers to you rather than someone with the same name. Record the URL.

(b) Restrict the search by including some keywords that denote your interests or something about you. Record the number of hits as before, and write down the URL of a relevant link.

(c) Locate a white pages site such as www.whitepages.co.uk and search for people with your name. Record how many entries, and if possible find out information recorded about you.

Chapter 2 (week 2)

Email, compression and basic security

2.1   Using Outlook Express

Microsoft Outlook Express is the most commonly available email program, as it is packaged with the Windows Operating System. It can be used to send and receive email.

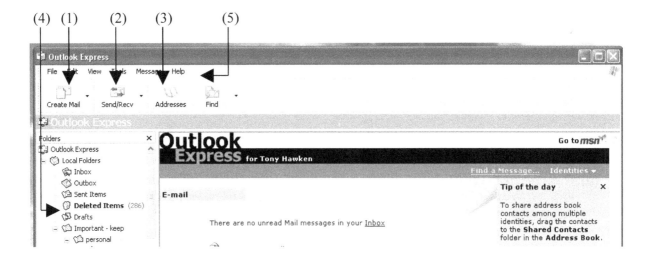

The following items will be considered:

1. Create Mail - used to create a new message

2. Send/Recv – Check for new mail or send mail

3. Address book – used to store details of contacts

4. Folders – used to organize mail

5. Menu bar – contains a number of pop-down menus

When you set up Outlook express for the first time there will be the following folders:

Inbox, Outbox, Sent Items, Deleted Items, Drafts

You can also create your own folders to organize your messages.

There are also a number of pop-down menus.

File — This contains options to open and save mail. You can also export individual messages or folders with messages. This is an important form of backup.

Edit — This includes important facilities such as Copy, delete and find

View — This includes facilities that determine how you view your messages. You can for instance sort them using different criteria, hide certain messages etc.

Tools — This option contains many useful tools. These include the address book, Accounts – which enables you to set up another email account or news etc, Options – this allows you to set up the properties of how mail is sent and received.

Message — This repeats the facilities that you have by clicking on the Reply, Reply All, and Forward buttons that are available when you read a message.

Help — provides you with help and tells you about your version of Microsoft Outlook Express.

2.2 Reading mail

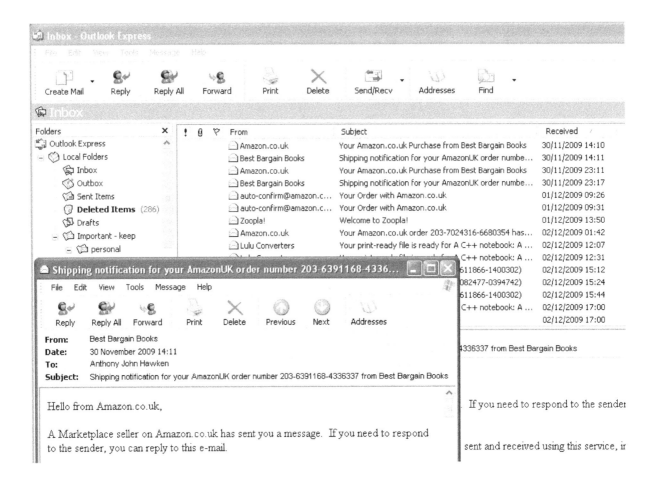

Mail can be read from the inbox by clicking on the inbox folder. To read a particular message click on a particular item listed. You can then use the following options:

Reply - Opens a copy of the current message so that you can edit it. When you click on send the modified message will be sent to the sender.

Reply All – Opens a copy of the current message so that you can edit it. When you click on send a copy will be sent to all recipients of the message as well as the sender.

Forward – this option is used if you want to sent the current message to someone else.

2.3   Creating and sending email

This facility is used to type in a message. You will need to enter the address of the person you intend to send the mail and also enter something for the subject indicating the nature of the message.

Then click on send, to send the message when you have finished.

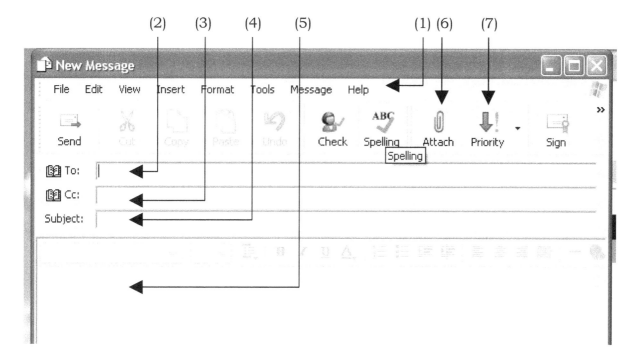

The following items are typically used for most email to be sent:

1. Menu bar - pop-down menus

2. To: - Enter email address here

3. Cc: - Carbon copy. Other people you wish to send a copy to

4. Subject: - An indication as to what the message is about

5. You type in the message here

6. Attachments are inserted below subject. Another Text box is created once you have inserted the first attachment

7. Priority – Important messages that need prompt attention should be marked priority. One of these messages will have a red exclamation mark next to it, indicating that it is urgent.

2.3.1   Send and Receive

This is used to check whether you have any incoming email. If you have this will be sent across from your ISP and will end up in your **Inbox** folder

This is also used to send email that is currently stored in your **Outbox** folder.

2.3.2   Menu bar

The menu bar includes some useful pop-down menus. The most useful being the following:

File	Send message using	- sends the current message
Insert	File attachment	- include a file of any type
	Text from file	- include text in mail message
	Picture	- insert picture in mail message

2.3.3   Inserting attachments

An **attachment** is a file that is attached to an email. The advantage of sending attachments is that they can be saved separately by the recipient of the email. Clicking on **File Attachment ...** will bring up a small window that will display files in the current folder – the last folder from which files were attached to an email. An alternative to this method is to click on the button with a paper clip (1). The recipient of this email will be able to spot that this email has an attachment, as there will be a paper clip alongside it in the list of emails in the inbox.

(1)

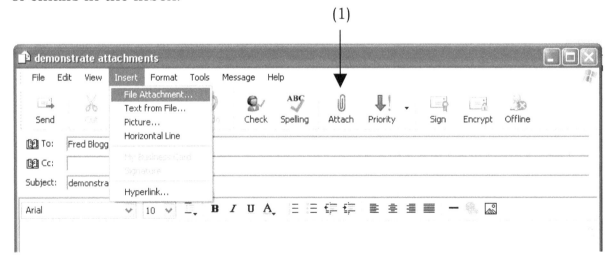

To identify a file to attach, you could enter the name of the file at (2), before clicking on Attach (3). However, you are more likely to want to browse for the

file you wish to insert as an attachment. To do this, click on the down arrow of the **Look in** pop-down menu (4). You will then see a list of folders.

If the file you want is somewhere on the E: drive double click on this item (6) and this entry will be expanded showing the folders on the E: drive. This can be repeated until you find the file you are looking for. You can restrict the type of file that you are looking for by clicking on (5).

Insert Attachment window showing contents of current folder

Insert Attachment Window showing folders on the computer.

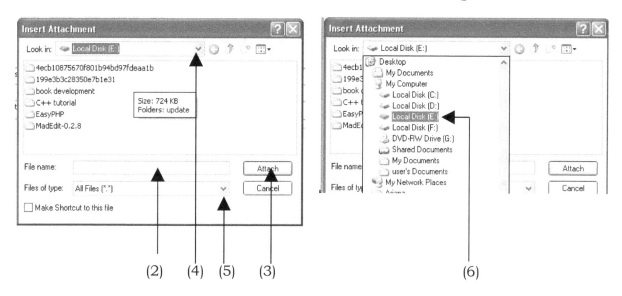

(2)   (4) (5)   (3)   (6)

2.3.4   Mail folders

There are five standard folders:

Inbox, Outbox, Sent items, deleted items and drafts

1. The **Inbox** is used to store received mail. It will stay in this folder until you delete it.

2. The **Outbox** contains mail that you wish to send. When the mail has been sent, it is also removed from the **Outbox** and a copy is deposited in the **Sent items** folder.

3. **Sent items** is a folder which contains mail that you have previously sent.

4. The **deleted** items folder contains mail deleted from other folders. To delete mail permanently you have to delete if from this folder also.

5. The **drafts** folder is used to store rough copies of email that you may send at a later date.

It is also possible to create your own folders if you have a lot of mail you wish to organize.

2.4   Address book

The address book is used to store email addresses and other details if required. Once details are entered, you can perform a search for an email address, or if the address book is small, you can scan the entire address book. In the picture below the e-mail addresses have been removed.

To create a new message intended for a particular sender, all you need to do is click on the name of the person in your address book.

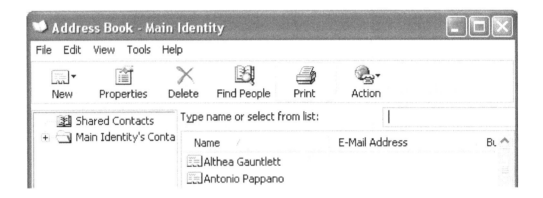

To add someone to your address book click on new contact. You will then be given a new window where you can add contact details. You should include name and email address. You can also include other details such as phone numbers.

A group is a list op people that you may want to send a message to simultaneously. Clicking on New group will create a new window, which will allow you list a group of people together.

Add a new contact

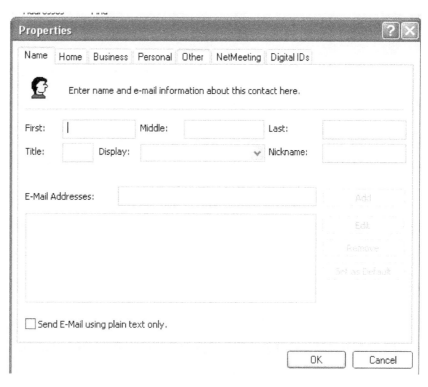

Add a new group

Once entries are entered in the address book, you can also create a group. This is often referred to as a mailing list or distribution list. It is merely a collection of address book entries that is given a name. After you have created a group you can add addresses to the group one at a time.

2.5   Using web mail

Web mail is the service you use if you have to log on to a particular account on a given web site. It is typically used by people who are away from their computer at home. So, if you are at college, or abroad you will have to use web mail. It is also used by people who do not have an ISP, and so cannot create a regular email mailbox.

2.5.1   Creating a hotmail account

Hotmail is one of the most popular providers of web mail. To create a hotmail account you need to use the MSN web site (http://uk.msn.com)

Click here to obtain hotmail

You will now obtain a new Window with the following. If you already have a hotmail account, you would enter your ID and password on the right-hand-side of the screen. Then click on Sign in.

If you are new to hotmail, you will need to click on Sign up.

Clicking on Sign up, opens up another window with a form for you to fill in. It looks like this. First of all you have to choose an ID (often based on your name). Having done this you click on the button "Check availability". If there is no one else using this name you can proceed, otherwise you will be required to change the ID. The rest of the form is self-explanatory. Just fill in the details, the same as you would any other form.

Create your Windows Live ID

It gets you into all Windows Live services—and other places you see ↵
All information is required.

ⓘ Already using **Hotmail**, **Messenger**, or **Xbox LIVE**? Sign in now

Windows Live ID:	[ ] @ [hotmail.co.uk ▾]
	[Check availability]
Create a password:	[ ]
	6-character minimum; case sensitive
Retype password:	[ ]
Alternate e-mail address:	[ ]
	Or choose a security question for password reset
First name:	[ ]
Last name:	[ ]
Country/region:	[United Kingdom ▾]
Constituent Country:	[Select one ▾]
Postal Code:	[ ]
Gender:	○ Male ○ Female
Birth year:	[Example: 1990]

45⁷³⁴⁷5L

☑ Send me e-mail with promotional offers and survey invitations from Windows Live, Bing, and MSN. (You can unsubscribe at any time.)

Characters: [   ]
Enter the 8 characters you see

Unless you want to receive unsolicited email from MSN, I suggest that you uncheck the box above.

The following shows a form that I have filled in. I have however for privacy erased the parts numbered (1) and (2). You would be expected to fill these in.

Notice that I have unchecked the check-box, so that I don't get unwanted email (3).

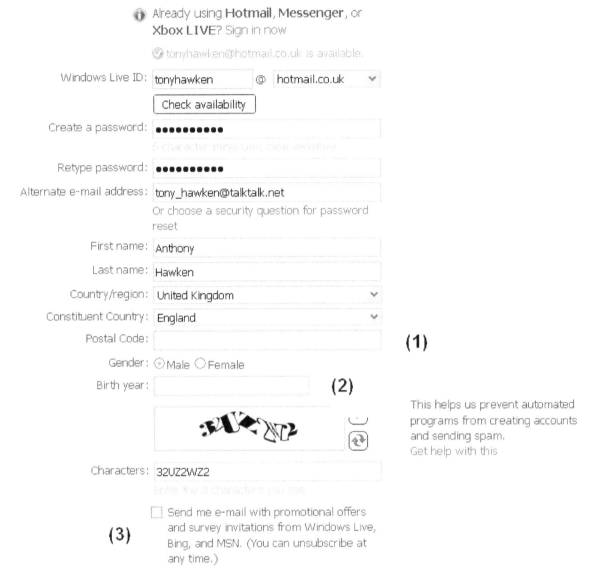

Finally, if you have successfully created a hotmail account you obtain the following with one message in the inbox. This tells you how to start using hotmail.

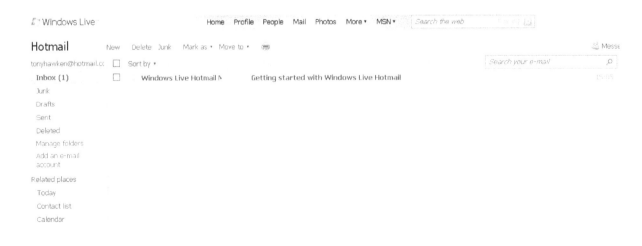

2.5.2   Using hotmail

You can use hotmail to do much the same as you would if you were using Microsoft Outlook Express. That is you need to be able to read mail, send mail and have the capability of organizing your messages.

When you log on, or have created an account for the first time you will obtain the following.

1. Folders. These contain different types of messages.

   Inbox – any mail you receive initially go here.
   Drafts – this folder is used to store incomplete messages that you will
           send later
   Sent –   copies of all messages sent by you are kept here.
   Deleted – copies of all deleted messages end up here.

2. New – used to create a new message

3. Delete – used to delete a message

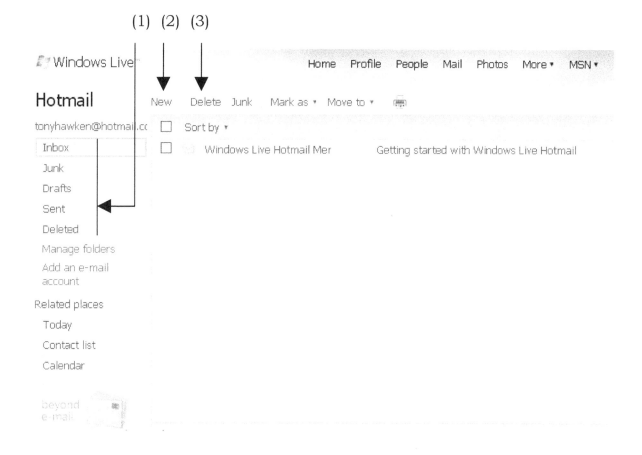

We will start by sending a simple message. In this case I will be sending a message to myself (My regular email account on my home computer).

2.5.3   Sending a message

To create a message, click on New. You then obtain the following.

The email address that you want to send the message, is entered in the text box labelled **To:**. In this case I enter tony_hawken@talktalk.net

It is important to enter a subject, so that the person who receives the message will have some idea what it is about.

And finally the message itself is entered.

When the message is complete, you click on **Send** to send it. When you do this, you will be asked to verify the message. You will be shown a number of distorted characters (similar in style to those when you logged on). You will then be expected to enter these characters. The idea behind this is, that if you have to verify messages like this, it is be used as a means of cutting down on spam.

2.5.4   Receiving mail

You can tell whether you have received email, as the number of unread messages in the Inbox increases. If you click on Inbox, all unread messages appear in bold. To read the message just click on any part of the message in bold.

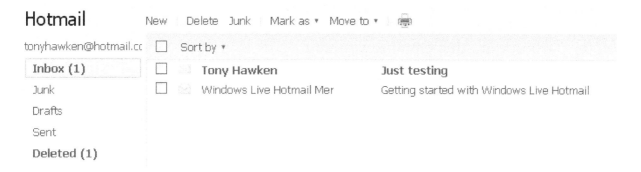

The picture below shows the message. In the header there is a subject name "Just testing". You can also find the name of the sender, the date sent, and the person to whom the mail was sent.

Below this is the message itself.

You will note that there are two buttons (1) "Mark as safe" and (2) "Mark as junk". If you are happy with this sender and you wish to continue receiving mail from this sender, click on "Mark as safe". All messages from this sender will then continue to be put in you inbox. However, if you click on "Mark as junk", further messages from this sender will be deposited in the Junk folder.

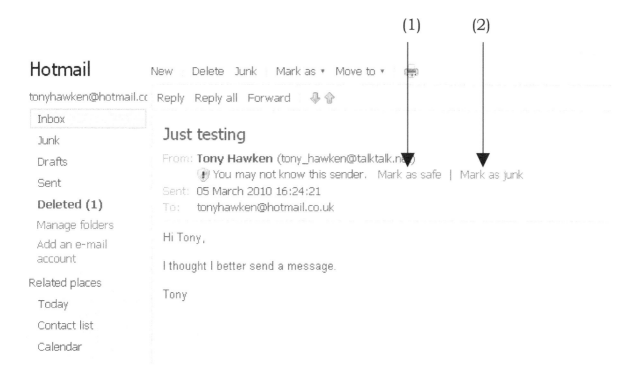

Exercise 2-1

1. The following tests a basic ability in using email. You will probably use Outlook Express, but you should be able to do the following using most email programs.

   (a) Send an email to tony_hawken@talktalk.net

   (b) Carbon copy this email to yourself

   (c) Include a message stating what you think of this book so far, and include details about the course you are studying, and the college where you are studying.

   (d) Insert an attachment of a picture. This could be a simple picture downloaded from the Internet. If the picture is small, also insert the picture in your message.

   (e) Send this message.

   (f) Go to the sent messages folder, locate and open this sent message. Obtain a screen dump to demonstrate that the message has been sent.

   (g) Enter this email address into your address folder.

   (h) Periodically check your email for a reply. When you obtain such a message in your inbox, obtain a screen dump of it.

   (i) Create a mail folder called Tony Hawken and move both messages to it.

2.5   File Compression

Files need to be compressed for a number of reasons. It they are smaller in size they can be transferred across the Internet in shorter time. Also, if you have a lot of small files in a folder, you can compress the folder and its contents, so that you only have one object to transfer. This zipped file can then be added as an attachment in an email for instance.

There are a number of file compression utilities that you can download for free or purchase. I chose to use ZipCentral as it is free and you can download it from the Internet. Other options include Winzip, PKZIP and WinRAR.

The picture below illustrates the process of compressing a folder with a number of files in it. First position the mouse pointer onto the file or folder that you wish to compress. In this case a folder called Text. If you right-click the mouse you obtain the pop-down menu shown. You could choose Add to Zip, or Add to "Text.zip". I chose to use Add to "Text.zip" as this is the easiest option.

Compress a folder or file, using pop-down menu from right-clicking

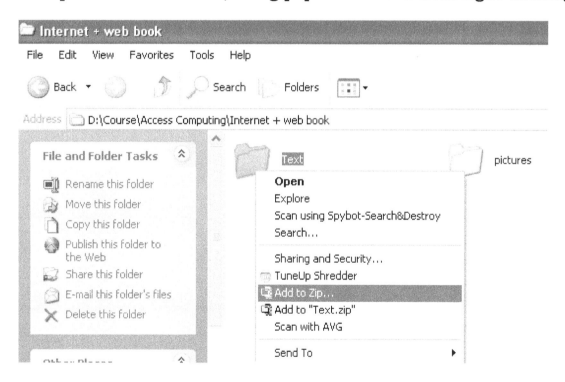

If you click on Add to "Text.zip" you have a number of options you can click on. For instance if the folder contains other folders, you will need to click on include subfolders. When you are satisfied with the options chosen, click on OK.

File compression options

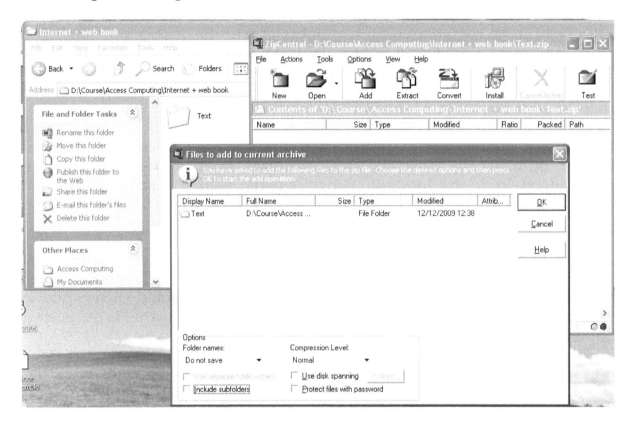

Once you have clicked on OK, ZipCentral will create an archive called Text.zip. Inside there will be the contents of the folder called Text. You will notice that the size of each file has been compressed.

The Zip archive

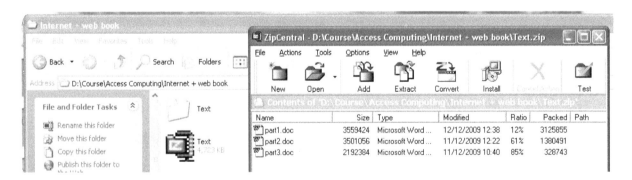

On the left is the icon for a ZipCentral archive. On the right-hand side is a window showing the contents for this particular zipped file.

To gain access (unzip the file) to a zipped file, you simply double click on the icon corresponding to the zipped file. You can then look at individual files within the archive by double-clicking them, or you can extract the archive by clicking on the button Extract. If you do this, all of the files will be copied to a new folder in the current folder, unless you specify that they should go somewhere else.

2.6 Using an anti-virus program

Nowadays it is essential to protect your computer, especially if you intend to use the Internet. A very popular product is AVG. A free version of this can be downloaded from the Internet. The image shown is that of AVG Internet Security. Other popular products include Norton Internet security, Kaspersky Internet Security and McAfee Total Protection.

This package contains an anti-virus program, a firewall, an email scanner, anti-spyware, and anti-spam facilities. This package usually detects viruses as they are introduced on to the computer. This is because the package is loaded onto the computer before most other software is loaded. It remains resident in memory and is continually on the lookout for files infected with viruses.

The anti-virus software should be active all the time, whilst the computer is switched on. It continually checks if new files are to be copied onto your computer. This usually happens when you are using the Internet or reading email (especially if there are attachments), and when you insert a CD or DVD into a drive on the computer.

Within this package you can use AVG anti-virus by clicking on the AVG icon. You would normally do this if you wanted to carry out a full system scan. You can also be more selective. That is you can choose to scan only certain drives or certain folders for viruses.

You should be doing a full system scan every week. Many people don't do this because it can take several hours.

The picture below shows a full system scan that has just started. The software usually starts scanning the most vulnerable part of the computer. That is, the drive and folders where most of the system files are located. It then continues looking at the rest of the hard-drive.

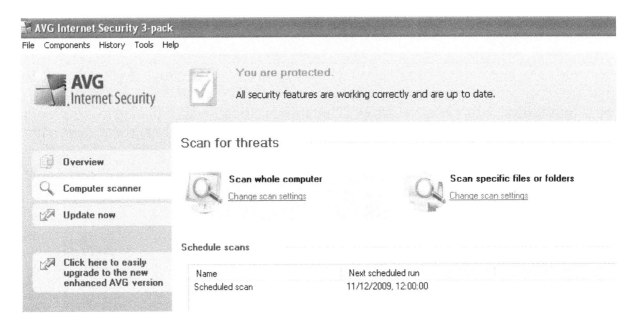

You can also selectively choose to scan individual files and folders. This is done by right-clicking on the object you wish to scan. Then choose the scan option. In the example below, I have right-clicked on the icon corresponding to a removable flash-memory drive. You should consider scanning these devices every time you plug one into your computer.

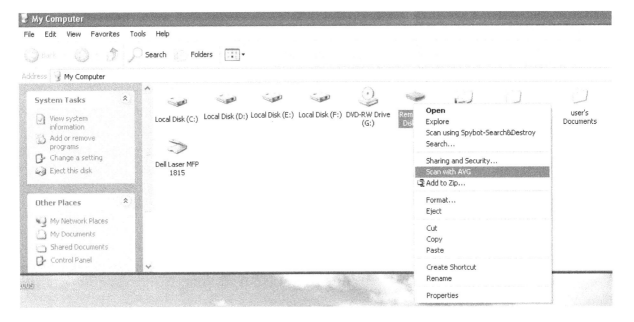

As well a these forms of security you should also be considering the use of one or more anti-spyware programs.

2.7 Using anti-spyware

Spyware is the term given to the group of malicious software (malware) that installs itself on people's computers and tracks information about them. They are a significant threat to ones privacy as they can be used to collect personal information such as your web browsing habits, and the sites you have visited. Spyware often affects your speed of Internet access, and often includes unwanted adverts (adware) and annoying pop-up windows. Most spyware is picked up by downloading software from the Internet. So, you should be really careful which sites you use to download software.

There are many anti-spyware programs available. Many of them can be downloaded from the Internet. Spybot is one of the most popular free programs that can be downloaded from the Internet. As well as tracking the less harmful spyware discussed above, it can also detect tojans (That are used to gain access to your computer) and keyloggers that are used to obtain personal information such as passwords.

Spybot is very easy to install and use. Typically each time you run the program, you should search for updates, as new versions of spyware are continually being produced. The option Search for Updates downloads the latest information from the Internet and typically only takes a couple of minutes at the most. You just need to click on Search for updates to start this process.

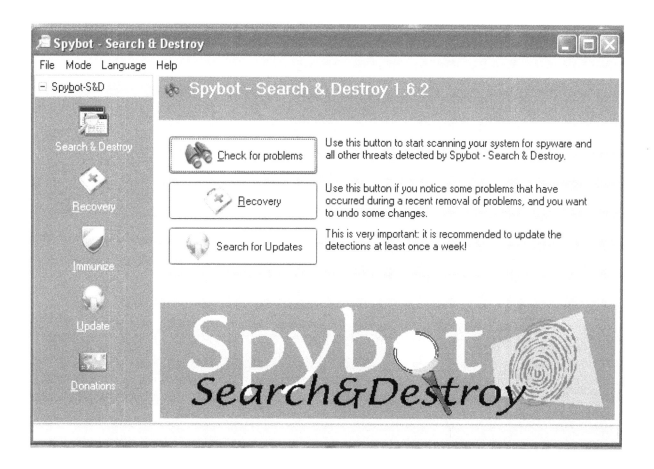

51

Once you have chosen the site where you wish to obtain your updates, you get a window like the one below indicating what updates are available for update. Those you want to include can be added by ticking the check-box if it hasn't been done already. Then click on download.

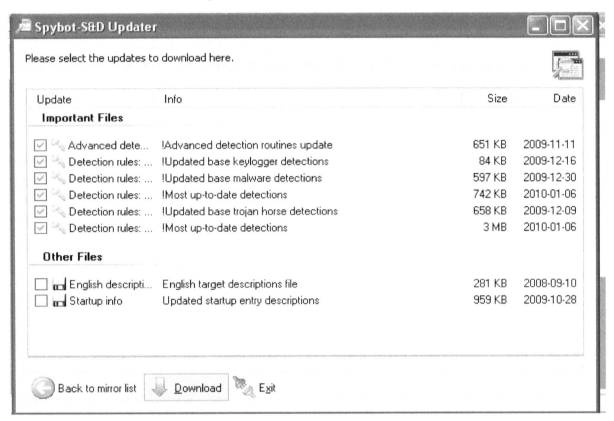

To scan for spyware, you now click on Check for problems. When the scan is finished you click on Fix selected problems.

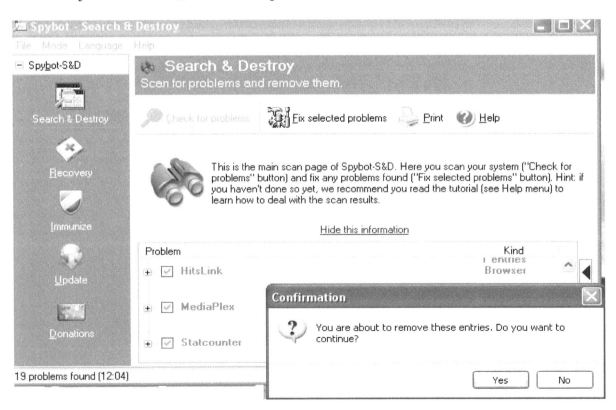

2.8   Browser settings and Internet security

You are always vulnerable to threats when you use a browser such as Internet Explorer to search for items on the Internet. You can however change both the security and privacy settings for Internet explorer.

You first need to click on the menu Tools, and from this pop-down menu click on Internet Options.

To change the security options, you first need to click on the Security tab. The easiest way to change the security settings is to move the slider(1). You can use this slider to determine the level of security (anywhere between Low and High). In some instances if your settings are too high, there will be some things that you will be unable to do on the Internet. Too low, then you become very vulnerable to attack.

In a similar manner, you can change the privacy settings. First you need to select the privacy tab, then move slider (2).

Security options   **Privacy options**

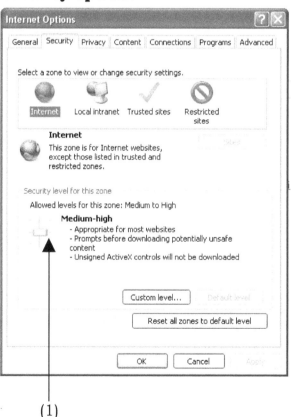

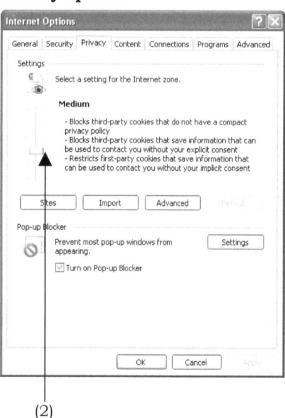

(1)   (2)

In both cases you will be told what the changes will be. For a beginner this is the best way to adjust your settings. A more advanced computer user will probably used the advanced settings, by clicking on the Advanced tab. This allows a user to change settings by clicking on checkboxes for each entry. The advanced tab contains Security, privacy and other properties.

Security options for Firefox

The security settings at a basic level can be set by first clicking on the security tab, then by checking the boxes for the settings you want,

In the case of the top 3 options chosen, a warning will be given if the event occurs. You will have the option whether to go ahead or block the action.

Privacy options for Firefox

A cookie is a small text file that a web server requests you to put on your computer. It contains personal information including your name, email address and IP address. This is useful to the site if you are returning to go shopping again etc.

The last two options that have been checked allow you to wipe all the private data collected, including the history of the web sites that you have visited

Clear Private data

This window pops up when you exit Mozilla Firefox if the privacy options are as above.

Here you can click on check boxes to specify the type of data that you want to clear. Once you have done this click on **Clear Private Data Now**. If you change your mind and don't want to clear the private data, click on Cancel.

Exercise 2-2

1. File compression

   (a) Using a search engine obtain links to ZipCentral. Click on a link where you can download the software.

   (b) Download and Install ZipCentral.

   (c) Create a zip archive of your folder that contains your current work. You could do this by right-clicking the folder you wish to compress. Find out what the compression rate is for different files in this archive.

   (d) Enter the URL:
   http://www.mathcs.richmond.edu/~hubbard/Books.html

   (e) Select the first book "Data Structures with Java" and click on the link "Source code". Save the file to a folder on your computer.

   (f) Extract the files in this zip archive.

2. Anti-virus

   (a) If you don't have an anti-virus program installed on your computer, enter the URL: http://www.avg.com/gb-en/download-trial .

   (b) Describe the facilities available in AVG Internet Security.

   (c) Download and Install AVG Internet Security trial version.

   (d) Obtain the latest updates.

   (e) Scan your computer for threats.

   (f) Insert a flash memory stick into a usb port of you computer. Scan the drive corresponding to the flash memory stick.

3. Anti-spyware

   (a) Enter the URL:
   http://www.safer-networking.org/en/download/index.html

   (b) Click on the link to download Spybot – Search & Destroy.

   (c) Install this software and obtain the latest updates. Then perform a full scan of your computer. Provide a screen dump of the results.

Chapter 3 (week 3)

Internet protocols and how the Internet works

3.1   Internet protocols

Use of the Internet is dependent on two very important protocols. These are TCP (Transmission control protocol) and IP (Internet protocol). The two protocols are often grouped together and referred to as TCP/IP. TCP/IP contains many other protocols used by Internet users.

Most modern operating systems provide TCP/IP access. In particular the following or similar programs are included as part of the operating system application software:

1. FTP (File Transfer Protocol). This is used to send files from one computer to another.

2. HTTP (Hypertext transfer protocol). This is the protocol used to access documents on the world-wide-web. It enables applications that use hypertext.

3. SMTP (Simple Mail Transfer Protocol). This provides the basic facilities to use email at all. This protocol has traditionally been limited to text-based electronic messages. It is used to transfer outgoing mail.

4. POP (Post office protocol) and POP3 is used for transferring incoming messages.

5. MIME (Multi-purpose Internet Mail Extension). It is this protocol which enables you to have better facilities when using email. For example you can attach Word documents and pictures to your email.

6. TELNET. Allows you to log on to a remote computer, and hence use the resources of that computer.

7. PING (**P**acket **IN**ternet **G**opher) - tells you whether a computer is available to access over the network.

Microsoft Windows 95 and later versions of the Windows operating system provide all of these facilities. In particular you can use the **ftp**, **telnet** and **ping** programs by making use of the Run facility. Alternatively you can run the command prompt (usually found in accessories), then enter the command you want to use.

3.2 How the Internet works

The following is a brief discussion about how the Internet works. In particular how data can be transferred from one computer to another.

3.2.1 client-server model

The Internet and networks in general use the client-server model. The person browsing the Internet is the client. The client software they are running on their computer is called a web browser. The job of the client software is to request information from the server. The server then obtains the requested page and sends it to the client computer

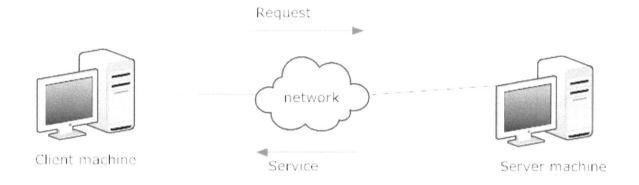

3.2.2 IP addresses

IP stands for **Internet protocol**. Each computer connected to the Internet has a unique address called its IP address. This is a sequence of 4 numbers. Each of the numbers takes up one byte of storage. So the numbers can be in the range 0-255. So for instance the IP address for www.croydon.ac.uk is 89.151.106.135 .

The format of an IP address is inconvenient for humans to read. That is why symbolic names are used in place of this set of numbers. Each node on the Internet has its IP address determined by the **Domain Name System** (DNS). **DNS** is a distributed database that translates Internet addresses (**Domain names**) to IP addresses. This is a bit like a telephone directory, but instead of telephone numbers, IP numbers are associated with Domain names.

3.2.3 Transfer of data

TCP/IP is made up of two main parts and contains about 100 different protocols. TCP allows computers on the Internet communicate with each other. IP is concerned with how data is routed from one computer to another.

Data that is to be sent from one computer to another is first split into IP packets. Within each packet there is some data from the original file and also control information. The control data includes a checksum that can be used to check whether data has been corrupted. Each packet also has a sequence number so that they can be reassembled in the correct order.

These packets are quite small. The advantage of small packets is that if data is lost, only a small amount needs to be re-sent. Also, if part of network is congested, it is easier to have the packet re-routed.

When the packets are received at the destination they are reassembled. If there are any packets missing or corrupted, a message is sent from the destination computer to the sending computer to re-send the necessary packets.

3.2.4   Retrieving a web page

Suppose I were to enter the URL: http://www.croydon.ac.uk/contact.html into the address bar of a web browser.

1. The browser will determine that a web page is requested, as the URL begins http.

2. Using the location part of the URL, the browser queries the DNS to translate this name into an IP address. In this case the IP address is 89.151.106.135 .

3. The browser now creates a TCP connection to 89.151.106.135 using port 80, which is the default port for web servers.

4. The browser now sends a message asking for the file contact.html. Often the filename will include the name of the folder that the file is stored in.

5. The server services this request by sending the file contact.html to the client computer.

6. The TCP connection is then closed, thus ending the communication between these two computers.

7. The browser interprets the text and HTML code and formats the text on the screen accordingly.

8. If there are any images in the html document, these steps are repeated to download these images as well.

3.3   How email works

To understand how you can send and receive email, we first have to discuss some key terms.

A **mailer** – also called a mail client, is the program that allows you to read, create and send mail. Eg Microsoft Outlook Express.

A **mail server** – is a dedicated computer that receives, stores, and delivers email. A server needs to be on and running nearly all the time.

A **mail box** is a file on your computer specifically for storing email. Mail boxes are created when you create a mail account – typically using Outlook Express (or whatever your mailer is).

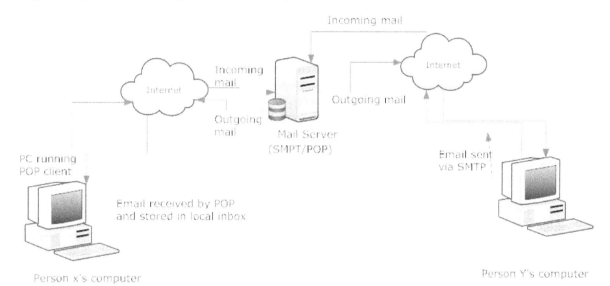

The mail server shown above has mailboxes for both X and Y. If person Y wants to send email to person X, first a message is composed using their mailer. It is temporarily stored in a local outbox. When the message is sent, it is transferred via SMTP to an inbox belonging to person X on the server.

When person X runs their mailer it indicates that there is mail to collect. For Microsoft Outlook Express, this usually happens each time you run the program, and also when you click on send/receive. The email is transferred using POP. This involves the message being downloaded to their computer and the message being deposited in a local inbox.

Exercise 3-1

1. Fill in the blanks in the following passages with these words: TCP/IP, HTTP, FTP, URL, TELNET, IP address, IP packet, DNS, mailer, mail server, mail box.

All computers connected to the Internet uses a group of protocols called _____. Each computer can be distinguished by 4 one-byte numbers called its _____. TCP/IP is made up of a lot of separate protocols. The protocol for transferring files from one computer is called _____. There is a _____ command that will enable you to transfer files. If however, you want to log onto another computer remotely you use the _____ protocol.

To download a web page, you could enter a _____ at the address bar. Because you are requesting a web page, it uses the _____ protocol. The address that you have entered needs to be converted to a sequence of numbers called its _____. The browser needs to use _____ to do this.

If you send someone email, the message you send uses the _____ protocol. This protocol is responsible for the message being stored in a _____ on a reliable computer called a _____. When the recipient of the email loads their _____, they are able to receive mail from the _____. This mail is then transferred to their local _____.

3.4   FTP commands

The following ftp commands are typical of programs that provide a command line interface.

Basic commands	
bye	quit the **ftp** program
?	list all the ftp commands
? command	summarize a particular command
help	display a list of all ftp commands
help command	summarize a particular command
Connecting	
open host	Connect to a remote computer (called host)
close	Close the connection to remote host.
Directories	
cd directory	change to a different directory on the remote machine
cdup	change to parent directory on the remote machine
dir [directory [local file]]	display a long directory listing of directory on remote machine
lcd directory	change directory on local machine
ls [directory [local file]]	get short directory listing on remote machine
pwd	display name of current directory on remote machine
Transferring files	
get remote-file	copies remote file to current directory
mget remote-files	copies remote files to current directory
put local-file	copies local file to current directory on remote machine
mput	copies many files to current directory on remote machine
Setting options	
ascii	Set file type to ASCII. This is the default
binary	Set file type to binary.

3.5 Downloading files using the ftp program

You can run FTP by entering **ftp** in the Run pop-down menu as follows:

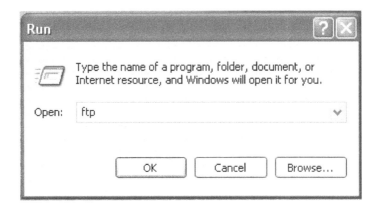

When you run ftp, you get a prompt like this:

ftp>

You can now enter ftp commands at this prompt. The following illustration uses ftp to list all of the ftp commands. In this case help has been entered to list the ftp commands.

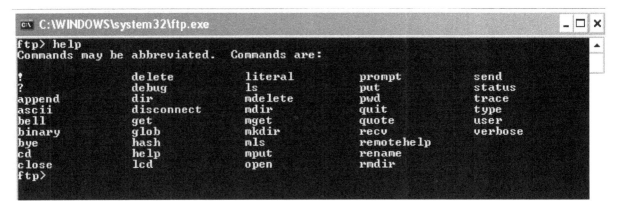

These facilities have been available within unix systems for the past 20 years or more and represented the only way you could use ftp to transfer files. There are also many freeware or shareware versions of ftp programs.

Typically you start an ftp session by running the ftp program, and using the **open** command to connect to a particular computer. You then typically use **get** and **put** commands to transfer files. It is assumed that when you transfer files, that they will be **text files**. If you know that you are going to transfer other types of file such as executable programs, you need to set the file type to **binary**. If you don't do this, you cannot expect the files to be transferred correctly. The file type **ascii** is used to specify text files, and is the default. Finally when you have finished on a particular computer you enter **close** or **quit** to finish the session.

In the next example I will be demonstrating how to connect to an ftp site, obtain a directory listing, change directory etc.

1. Run the ftp program

2. Connect to the site. Enter the command **open ftp.gnu.org**

```
C:\WINDOWS\system32\ftp.exe
ftp> open ftp.gnu.org
Connected to ftp.gnu.org.
220 GNU FTP server ready.
User (ftp.gnu.org:(none)): _
```

3. Logon to the site as user **anonymous.** This username does not require a password.

```
C:\WINDOWS\system32\ftp.exe                                              _ [
ftp> open ftp.gnu.org
Connected to ftp.gnu.org.
220 GNU FTP server ready.
User (ftp.gnu.org:(none)): anonymous
230-Due to U.S. Export Regulations, all cryptographic software on this
230-site is subject to the following legal notice:
230-
230-      This site includes publicly available encryption source code
230-      which, together with object code resulting from the compiling of
230-      publicly available source code, may be exported from the United
230-      States under License Exception "TSU" pursuant to 15 C.F.R. Section
230-      740.13(e).
230-
230-This legal notice applies to cryptographic software only. Please see
230-the Bureau of Industry and Security (www.bxa.doc.gov) for more
230-information about current U.S. regulations.
230 Login successful.
ftp>
```

Entering the command **dir** at the ftp> prompt gives the following listing.

```
C:\WINDOWS\system32\ftp.exe                                          _ 🗗 ×
230-information about current U.S. regulations.
230 Login successful.
ftp> dir
200 PORT command successful. Consider using PASV.
150 Here comes the directory listing.
lrwxrwxrwx    1 0            0               8 Aug 20   2004 CRYPTO.README -> .messag
e
-rw-r--r--    1 0            0           17864 Oct 23   2003 MISSING-FILES
-rw-r--r--    2 0            0            4178 Aug 13   2003 MISSING-FILES.README
-rw-r--r--    1 0            0            1765 Feb 20   2007 README
-rw-r--r--    1 0            0          405121 Oct 23   2003 before-2003-08-01.md5sum
s.asc
-rw-r--r--    1 0            0          157549 Mar 05 11:36 find.txt.gz
drwxrwxr-x  294 0         1003            8192 Mar 03 19:30 gnu
drwxrwxr-x    3 0         1003            4096 Sep 23   2004 gnu+linux-distros
-rw-r--r--    1 0            0              90 Feb 16   1993 lpf.README
-rw-r--r--    1 0            0          325396 Mar 05 11:36 ls-lrRt.txt.gz
drwxr-xr-x    3 0            0            4096 Apr 20   2005 mirrors
lrwxrwxrwx    1 0            0              11 Apr 15   2004 non-gnu -> gnu/non-gnu
drwxr-xr-x   53 0            0            4096 Jan 10 18:01 old-gnu
lrwxrwxrwx    1 0            0               1 Aug 05   2003 pub -> .
drwxr-xr-x    2 0            0            4096 Nov 08   2007 savannah
drwxr-xr-x    2 0            0            4096 Aug 02   2003 third-party
drwxr-xr-x    2 0            0            4096 Apr 07   2009 tmp
drwxr-xr-x    2 0            0            4096 Dec 29 20:48 video
-rw-r--r--    1 0            0             954 Aug 13   2003 welcome.msg
226 Directory send OK.
ftp: 1332 bytes received in 0.00Seconds 1332000.00Kbytes/sec.
ftp>
```

You can change directory by using the **cd** command. You can then list the contents of the directory using **dir** again, and then identify the files that you wish to transfer. In this example we have changed to directory gnu.

```
ftp> cd gnu
250-If you have problems downloading and are seeing "Access denied" or
250-"Permission denied", please make sure that you started your FTP client
250-in a directory to which you have write permission.
250-
250-Please note that all files ending in '.gz' are compressed with 'gzip',
250-not with the unix 'compress' program. Get the file below for more
250-info.
250-
250-For a list of mirrors and other ways of getting GNU software, FTP the
250-file /pub/gnu/GNUinfo/FTP from ftp.gnu.org or one of its mirror sites.
250-
250-Programs that are directly in this directory are actually GNU
250-programs, developed under the auspices of GNU.
250-
250-We do, however, distribute some non-GNU programs through our FTP
250-server, or provide pointers to where they are. We put these
250-programs/pointers in the subdirectory non-gnu since they are not
250-developed by the GNU project. They are, of course, part of the GNU
250-system. See:
250-http://www.gnu.org/philosophy/categories.html#TheGNUsystem
250 Directory successfully changed.
ftp> _
```

The following illustration shows part of the directory listing. On the left-hand-side you have the access permissions for each file. Those that start with a d are directories. The access permissions r, w, and x stand for read , write and execute respectively.

```
drwxrwxr-x   2 0      1003        4096 Jun 20  2009  cpio
drwxrwxr-x   2 0      1003        4096 Aug 02  2003  cpp2html
drwxr-xr-x   2 1003   1003        4096 Mar 03 19:30  cppi
drwxr-xr-x   2 1003   1003        4096 Apr 11  2009  cssc
drwxrwxr-x   2 0      1003        4096 Feb 21  2008  dap
-rw-r--r--   1 1003   65534        110 Jun 06  1999  dc.README
drwxrwxr-x   2 0      1003        4096 Feb 11  2009  ddd
drwxr-xr-x   2 1003   1003        4096 Jul 10  2009  ddrescue
drwxrwxr-x   2 0      1003        4096 Jan 30  2004  dejagnu
drwxr-xr-x   2 1003   1003        4096 Mar 04 06:40  denemo
-rw-r--r--   1 1003   65534        145 May 22  2001  dia.README
drwxr-xr-x   2 1003   1003        4096 Mar 31  2009  dico
drwxrwxr-x   2 0      1003        4096 Sep 17  2007  diction
-rw-r--r--   1 1003   65534        134 Apr 15  2002  dictionary.README
drwxrwxr-x   2 0      1003        4096 Feb 13 13:10  diffutils
drwxr-xr-x   2 1003   1003        4096 Nov 28 19:00  dionysus
drwxrwxr-x   2 0      0           4096 Apr 03  2007  dismal
-rw-r--r--   1 1003   65534        492 Apr 03  2007  djgpp.README
drwxr-xr-x   2 1003   1003        4096 Feb 18  2005  dominion
drwxrwxr-x   5 0      1003        4096 Dec 10  2008  dotgnu
-rw-r--r--   1 1003   65534         96 Feb 09  1999  dumb.README
drwxrwxr-x   2 0      1003        4096 Jul 10  2009  ed
drwxrwxr-x   2 0      1003        4096 Aug 02  2003  edma
drwxrwxr-x   2 0      1003        4096 Feb 12 00:20  electric
```

Finally we copy a file to the current directory.

```
250 Directory successfully changed.
ftp> get g++.readme
200 PORT command successful. Consider using PASV.
550 Failed to open file.
ftp>
```

3.6   Download files using ftp (using a browser)

In the above example the URL: ftp://anarres.cs.berkeley.edu/pub/ has been entered in the address bar of Mozilla Firefox. You will notice that there is a long list of folders. If you double click on any of these folders, you will move to that folder.

In the image above, you will notice that I have double clicked the folder geometry. In it there is a single file. As it happens to be a text file, if you double click on this it will open the file in notepad. If there file format were zip, exe, or pdf etc, you would also have the option of saving the file.

3.7 Uploading files using ftp (Using a browser)

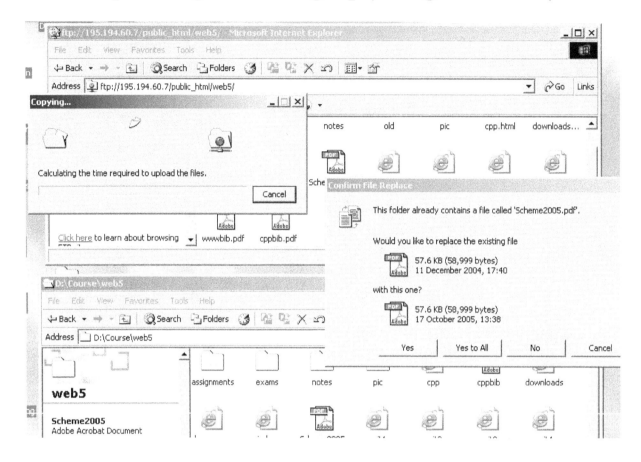

Uploading is the reverse of downloading. That is you copy files from your computer to the server where the web pages are located. In the example above the file Scheme2005.pdf is copied from a folder called Web5 on my computer to the access-computing web-space at Croydon college. This is achieved by dragging the appropriate icon and dropping it into the folder where the web-space is located.

In detail this was achieved as follows:

• Log on to the internet

• Enter the URL of the ftp site where you wish to upload files (Need a password for this)

• Double-click on the required folder where you wish to upload the files

• Locate file to upload. Open folder where it is to be found.

• Click on required file, and drag it to the window with the ftp site.

• After a while a window will open, indicating the progress of the copying.

3.8   Dealing with common problems

If you cannot connect to a given web-site, it is often necessary to use other programs within the TCP/IP protocol to investigate what is happening.

ping

The ping (Packet Internet Gopher) program determines whether a host computer is responding. It is typically used to trace problems in networks and uses the ICMP (Internet Control Message Protocol). It can also be used to determine delays in transfer, as the time for each reply is given in milliseconds.

If the host computer is active there is a reply indicating that you have successfully communicated with the host computer. If you get a message indicating failure, this could be for one of two reasons.

1. The host computer has network problems.
2. The host computer has blocked ping, because ping can be used to hack computers.

```
Command Prompt                                              _ □ ×

C:\>ping www.microsoft.com

Pinging lb1.www.ms.akadns.net [207.46.19.190] with 32 bytes of data:

Request timed out.
Request timed out.
Request timed out.
Request timed out.

Ping statistics for 207.46.19.190:
    Packets: Sent = 4, Received = 0, Lost = 4 (100% loss),

C:\>_
```

In the above, the request have timed out. This is probably because Microsoft do not want people to use **ping** on their site.

```
Command Prompt                                              _ □ ×

C:\>ping www.google.co.uk

Pinging www-tmmdi.l.google.com [216.239.59.103] with 32 bytes of data:

Reply from 216.239.59.103: bytes=32 time=43ms TTL=51
Reply from 216.239.59.103: bytes=32 time=42ms TTL=51
Reply from 216.239.59.103: bytes=32 time=42ms TTL=51
Reply from 216.239.59.103: bytes=32 time=44ms TTL=51

Ping statistics for 216.239.59.103:
    Packets: Sent = 4, Received = 4, Lost = 0 (0% loss),
Approximate round trip times in milli-seconds:
    Minimum = 42ms, Maximum = 44ms, Average = 42ms

C:\>
```

In the previous example, ping has been successful. Here replies are evident; all information sent has been received.

nslookup

The nslookup program checks the local hosts file or a DNS server to determine the IP address of an Internet node. If it can't find it in the local file it communicates with DNS servers outside its own network to see if they know the address.

```
C:\>nslookup www.microsoft.com
Server:  www.routerlogin.com
Address:  192.168.1.1

Non-authoritative answer:
Name:    lb1.www.ms.akadns.net
Addresses:  64.4.31.252, 207.46.19.190, 207.46.19.254
Aliases:  www.microsoft.com, toggle.www.ms.akadns.net
          g.www.ms.akadns.net

C:\>_
```

tracert

The tracert program can be used to trace the route of an IP packet through the Internet. It attempts to get a response from each of the intermediate gateways along the path towards the target host.

```
C:\>tracert www.google.co.uk

Tracing route to www-tmmdi.l.google.com [216.239.59.103]
over a maximum of 30 hops:

  1     *        *        *     Request timed out.
  2    28 ms    29 ms    29 ms  92.24.160.1
  3    29 ms    29 ms    29 ms  78.151.234.3
  4    30 ms    28 ms    30 ms  xe-11-0-0-rt001.bre.as13285.net [78.151.225.35]

  5    30 ms    29 ms    29 ms  62.24.240.37
  6    30 ms    29 ms    29 ms  xe-11-2-0-scr001.sov.as13285.net [78.144.1.130]

  7    29 ms    29 ms    30 ms  xe-11-3-0-scr010.sov.as13285.net [78.144.0.221]

  8   113 ms    31 ms    30 ms  google-pp-sov.as13285.net [78.144.5.6]
  9    32 ms    29 ms    29 ms  209.85.255.175
 10    46 ms    42 ms    44 ms  209.85.250.216
 11    44 ms    42 ms    42 ms  66.249.95.169
 12    56 ms    53 ms    53 ms  216.239.49.126
 13    43 ms    44 ms    44 ms  gv-in-f103.1e100.net [216.239.59.103]

Trace complete.

C:\>
```

Exercise 3-2

1. Fill in the blanks in the following passage with these words:

    telnet, ftp, nslookup, traceroute, IP, DNS, TCP/IP, ftp

    The protocol _____ is used by all computers connected to the Internet. Most operating systems have built-in networking commands that use the _____ protocol. One such command that is used to determine the _____ address of a computer is _____. This command uses _____ to obtain the _____ when a given Domain name is entered. To determine the route taken to get to a site, you would use the _____ command. You can log on to a remote computer using the _____ command. One of the oldest networking utilities that precedes the Internet is _____; this is used to transfer files from one computer to another.

2. Use the ping command to find out whether the following nodes are responding:

    (a) www.grisoft.com
    (b) www.yahoo.com
    (c) www.amazon.co.uk

3. Determine the IP addresses for the following sites:

    (a) www.amazon.co.uk
    (b) www.wmin.ac.uk
    (c) www.stanford.edu

4. Determine if possible the route taken from your computer to the following locations:

    (a) www.microsoft.co.uk
    (b) www.amazon.com
    (c) www.google.co.uk

5. An exercise in using ftp

    (a) Enter the URL ftp://ftp.gnu.org into the address bar of your browser

    (b) Double click the folder gnu

    (c) Within the folder gnu, double click the folder windows

    (d) Within the folder windows double click the folder emacs

    (e) Double click on the file emacs-22.3barebin-i386.zip, and when prompted save it in a folder on your computer

Chapter 4 (week 4)

An example assignment

4.1 Sample assignment brief

Access Computing

Assignment for unit 1

Using the Internet and email

In this assignment you will demonstrate your knowledge about using the Internet. You will also use the Internet to conduct research about the Logo Programming language.

Task 1

Create a directory called **Internet** and create a Microsoft WORD document called "Task 1" that includes the following.

(a) Define the terms - Internet, world-wide-web, search engine, directory, web-browser.

(b) Describe 3 general-purpose search engines and 3 specialist search engines. For each example given, include a URL.

(c) Describe the following Internet protocols - HTTP, FTP, SMTP, MIME, TELNET.

Task 2

Use a search engine to locate the following resources.

(a) Information about MSWLogo or StarLogo

(b) Sites that contain both MSWLogo and StarLogo

(c) Notes about Logo programming in PDF format

(d) Books about the Logo programming language

(e) Free Logo software

For each of the above, record the search engine used, the query entered, and the URL of a useful site located with this query. Where possible you should use a query that is specific and limits the hit-rate.

You will be required to provide evidence that all of these tasks have been achieved. A screen dump of the web page or file downloaded should suffice.

Task 3

Find out where you can obtain a drink in a pub in Penge. Obtain a map and get directions from Croydon college to one of these pubs. Get a screen dump of both the map and directions. Save the complete web page and also save a picture of an individual pub that you are considering to visit.

Task 4

(a) Send me an email that indicates your progress to date, and which requests further information to continue your research.

(b) Print a copy of your email, and a copy of the reply that will follow.

Task 5

(a) Enter the FTP address

ftp://ftp.cs.berkeley.edu

(b) Obtain a screen dump to show the folders present at this FTP site.

(c) Move to the ucb folder

(d) Move to ucblogo folder within this folder and download the file ucblogo60setup.exe into the **Internet** folder.

4.2 Task 1

This task can be done by reading sections of this book, reading sections of other books, or searching on the Internet. The references below are for this book.

Question a

Internet	–	see section 1.1 page 2
World wide web	–	see section 1.1 page 2
Search engine	–	see section 1.9 page 21
Directory	–	see section 5.2 page 80
Web browser	–	see section 1.1 page 3.

Question b

General purpose Search Engines

Choose from:

Google, yahoo, bing, ask Jeeves etc. Also see section 1.9 (Search Engines)

Special purpose Search Engines

This can include any site where a search engine is used to search for specific things. They can include shopping sites such as Amazon or ebay.

Question c

See section 3.1 (Internet protocols)

4.3   Task 2

a	Information about both MSW logo or starlogo Google "MSW logo" OR starlogo http://education.mit.edu/starlogo/	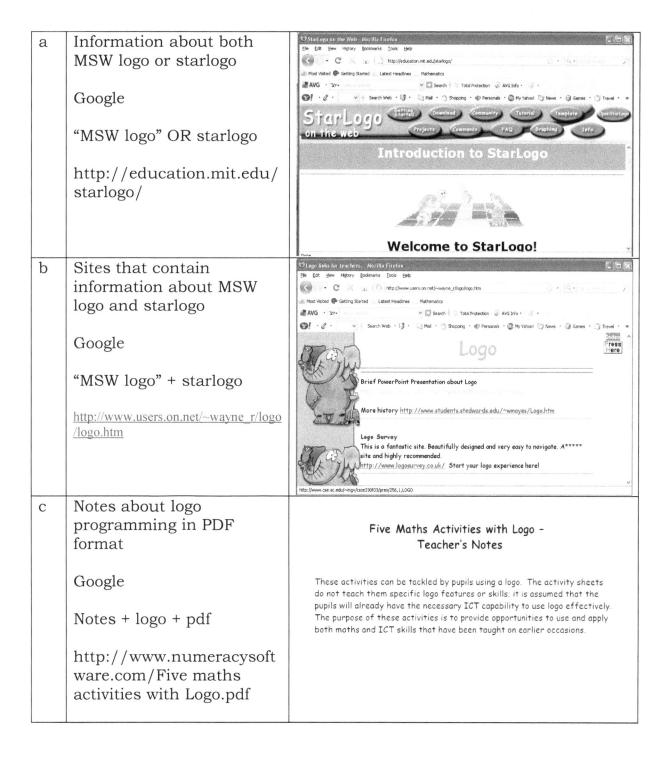
b	Sites that contain information about MSW logo and starlogo Google "MSW logo" + starlogo http://www.users.on.net/~wayne_r/logo/logo.htm	
c	Notes about logo programming in PDF format Google Notes + logo + pdf http://www.numeracysoftware.com/Five maths activities with Logo.pdf	Five Maths Activities with Logo – Teacher's Notes These activities can be tackled by pupils using a logo. The activity sheets do not teach them specific logo features or skills; it is assumed that the pupils will already have the necessary ICT capability to use logo effectively. The purpose of these activities is to provide opportunities to use and apply both maths and ICT skills that have been taught on earlier occasions.

d	Books about logo programming Google Books + "logo programming" http://www.softronix.com/logo.html	**Printed and Interactive Books** 📖 The Great Logo Adventure : Electronic copy of the actual book on learning Logo by Jim Muller (Graciously donated by Jim) 3.5 MB 📖 The Great Logo Adventure CD : All files on the accompanied CD included with the published book by Jim Muller 1.5 MB 📖 Computer Science Logo Style : a set of printed books on more advanced Logo programming techniques by Brian Harvey (bh@cs.berkeley.edu) 📖 A Turtle for the Teacher : a web based book on learning Logo by Paul Dench (paul.dench@bigpond.com.au) 📖 An Introduction to MSW Logo : a web based book on learning Logo by Jim Fuller (jfuller@southwest.com.au) 📖 Logo Lessons : a web based book on learning Logo by Michael Koss (mikeko@microsoft.com) 📖 Logo class outline : a web based class outline for Logo by Simon Rudge (srudge@yukoncollege.yk.ca)
e	Free logo software Google "Free logo software" http://www.worthytips.com/free-logo-programing-language-software-for-kids/	**Free Logo Programing Language Software For Kids** Posted on February 17, 2009 by Arafat Hossain Piyada ADVERTISEMENTS **Microsoft Courses** Work and learn at the same time Average salaries over £37k Career-in-IT.co.uk/programming **Computer Programming** Learn from Home in 2010 with the UKs Leading provider of IT Training Computeach.co.uk/programming **Custom MT4 Programming** Have your custom MT4 EA written. Conscientious, Personal Service. roycepipkins.com **It Course** It Course, Learn From Home IT & Computing Courses, Home Study www.HomeLearningCourses.com **Ads by Google** Software Developer Cumbria Programming Jobs Cumbria Freeware Restore Sample Programming Ads by Google Logo considers the first step of learning programming language for kids. There are too many kids school where Logo used to give the kids skill on programming language. There are both Free and Commercial version available on net now. Both GUI and DOS mood are available for general public. Here I listed some free Logo Software Provider's site link where you can download Logo Software Free.

4.4 Task 3

Map of Penge showing local pubs. This was obtained by clicking on maps. Then a query pub + penge was entered.

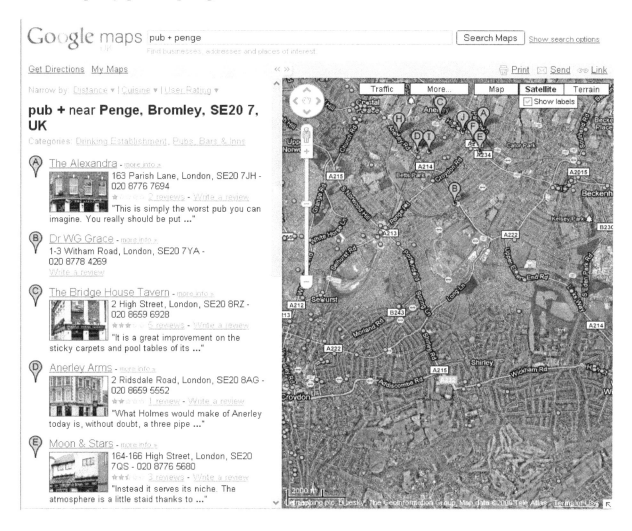

Clicking on icon E, pulls up some information about the pub. It also allows us to get instructions – how to get there.

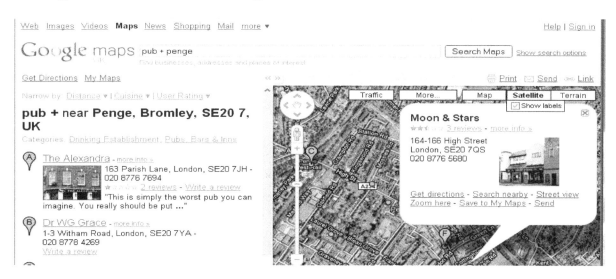

If you click on **Get directions**, then enter Croydon College, you can obtain the following map and directions of how to get to the pub from Croydon college.

4.5   Task 4

To do this exercise you will need to obtain the email address of two of you teachers. Also include yourself in the distribution list.

(a)   Get a screen dump of email that you sent

(b)   Get a screen dump of reply received.

4.6   Task 5

(b)   screen dump of ftp site

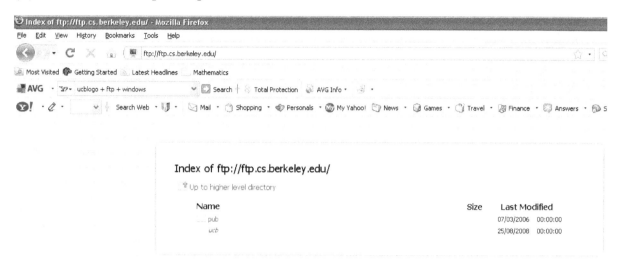

(c)   move to ucb folder - screen dump of ucb folder

(d)   move to ucblogo folder and download ucblogo60setup.exe

Index of ftp://ftp.cs.berkeley.edu/ucb/ucblogo/

⬆ Up to higher level directory

Name			
UCBLogo-6.0.dmg.gz			
UCBLogo-6.0.dmg.sitx			
UCBLogo.dmg.sitx			
bhtools.lwr			
blogo.exe			
blogo53.exe			
csls-errata	1 KB	08/07/2002	00:00:00
csls.tar.Z	66 KB	19/09/2000	00:00:00
csls.zip	47 KB	22/07/2004	00:00:00
logo-3.5		26/03/2003	00:00:00
old		25/11/2008	00:00:00
ucblogo-4.xo	2790 KB	14/09/2008	00:00:00
ucblogo-6.0.tar.gz	6538 KB	14/09/2008	00:00:00
ucblogo.sea	1538 KB	14/09/2008	00:00:00
ucblogo.sea.hqx	2122 KB	14/09/2008	00:00:00
ucblogo.tar.gz	6538 KB	14/09/2008	00:00:00
ucblogo53.sea	1538 KB	02/02/2003	00:00:00
ucblogo53.sea.hqx	2122 KB	02/02/2003	00:00:00
ucbwlogo60setup.exe	6864 KB	14/09/2008	00:00:00
ucbwlogosetup.exe	6864 KB	14/09/2008	00:00:00
usermanual	152 KB	14/09/2008	00:00:00

Opening ucbwlogo60setup.exe

You have chosen to open

ucbwlogo60setup.exe

which is a: Binary File
from: ftp://ftp.cs.berkeley.edu

Would you like to save this file?

[Save File]   [Cancel]

Chapter 5 (week 5)

Summary

5.1 Tasks to finish

This week is to be used to finish your coursework. At this stage you should have all the skills that you need to complete your coursework. I will include a basic list of tasks that will summarise what you need to do.

1. Collect the necessary information. If there is insufficient information in this book, you will have to borrow a book from the library. The bibliography at the end of this book has some useful suggestions. You could also consider searching for topics on the Internet.

2. Create a bibliography listing your sources of information. This should be one of the first tasks you do, as it helps you structure your report. Also, if you have to reference your sources of information, you already have it written down. Don't forget to include page numbers of books used. That way it will be easy to find the information again.

3. Much of the information required for an assignment task will come from the Internet. Create one or more folders to store this information. It is much better to save any possible useful documents obtained from the Internet rather than print them out. Only print out the most useful information. This copy can then be annotated.

4. Much of what you do in this module requires you to be able to search for and locate required information. You will have to demonstrate that you can formulate a query using Boolean operators.

5. You will also need to remember some basic computing skills. In particular you will be expected to know how to obtain screen dumps, crop them in paint and be able to insert them into a word-processed document. This is often required as evidence that the task has been achieved.

6. You will need to have a basic understanding of how web pages are retrieved and how email is sent and received. There is a very brief description in this book. There are further descriptions in a number of books and also on the Internet. You will also have to know what the main Internet protocols are for, but you are not expected to know details about their structure. You will also be expected to be able to use a number of programs associated with these protocols.

7. You will also need to demonstrate that you can use one or more email programs and that you have a basic knowledge about keeping your computer secure.

5.2   Unit Summary

1. Most people with a PC will already have all the software they require to log on to the Internet and access the web, as it is built into the Windows Operating System. These include utilities to make a connection to the Internet and software for transferring files such as FTP.

2. To browse the World Wide Web though you need to have access to a web browser. Most people will already be using Microsoft Internet Explorer as this comes packaged with the Windows operating system. You can however download other browsers from the Internet for free. The most popular alternative is Mozilla Firefox.

3. You can access a given web site in a number of ways. If you know the URL you can enter this at the address bar. If you don't, you can use a search engine to locate the web site you are looking for.

4. One of the most popular search engines is google. The UK version has the URL http://www.google.co.uk . It is normal to store this URL for your default homepage. That way you will start with google each time your browser is loaded. Your homepage can be changed using Internet Options if your browser is Internet Explorer.

5. A search engine makes a search for likely web sites based on an entered query. A simple query will consist of a single keyword. A more complex one will consist of a number of keywords joined with one or more of the Boolean operators AND, OR, and NOT. Different search engines represent these operators in different ways.

6. Another important application for the Internet is email. If you have an account with an ISP, it is quite likely that your default email client is Microsoft Outlook Express as this is packaged with the Windows Operating system. If you don't have an ISP you will have to sign up for a webmail account such as hotmail.

7. Email is one of the most common forms of communication. It is cheaper than using the telephone and has the advantage that you can send documents.

8. To carry out any type of online activity safely you need to have additional software installed on your computer. It is inconceivable that you would use your computer to access the Internet without having some sort of Anti-virus program. Most people opt for an integrated Internet security

package, that as well as an anti-virus program includes a firewall, anti-spam, anti-spyware etc.

9. A firewall is a program that controls access between one or more computers and the Internet. A firewall can check on incoming data from other computers and will reject it unless configured to accept it.

10. In addition to these precautions, you have to be aware that although the Operating System itself is vulnerable to attack, you can minimize this by altering your Browser settings. The idea is to remove facilities that pose a large degree of risk, whilst retaining those facilities that you really need.

11. Each computer on the Internet has a unique IP address. This is typically a set of numbers separated by decimal points. To make this address more meaningful to humans, each IP address is associated with a domain name that is made up of symbolic names.

12. A DNS (Domain Name Server) is responsible for translating Domain Names to IP addresses.

13. TCP/IP contains about 100 Internet protocols. It specifies how different computers should communicate with each other over the Internet. It includes such protocols as FTP to specify how files are to be transferred, HTTP that determines how browsers can access information from the World Wide Web, POP3 and SMTP that are used to determine how mail is sent and received.

14. Before the World Wide Web was invented, it was still possible to access the Internet, but in a much more primitive way. Typically everything was done at a command line. These same facilities for accessing the Internet from a command line still exist. You can still transfer files from one computer to another using FTP from a command line in much the same way as it was done before the World Wide Web existed.

15. The main protocols for using email are POP3 and SMTP. SMTP is used to specify how outgoing mail is to be sent. Whilst POP3 specifies how incoming mail is to be received. Both of the protocols work only for text-based messages. If you want to send or receive files in other formats, the MIME protocol is required.

16. To use email, 3 things are required. You need to have an email client such as Outlook Express installed on your computer. You also need to have created a mailbox. This is a file that is used to store email. You get one of these when you set up an email account. Your ISP needs to have a mail server. This is the software that is responsible for receiving mail, storing it, and sending it to the correct destination.

Part 2

Web Site Development (HTML)

Aims

After completing this 5-week unit, you will be able to do the following:

World Wide Web and HTML documents

Be able to describe what the world-wide-web is, how it developed, the applications that depend on it and why it is important.

Be able to view the source code of a web page.

Create simple web pages

Understand the basic structure of a web page, and be able to create web pages with the tags <HTML>, <HEAD>. <BODY>, <TITLE>, <P> and <BR>, and <H1> ... <H6> using a text editor.

Add different size headings to web pages.

Add a title to a web page

Presentation of text

Include tags to add emphasis to text - <B>, <U>, <I>, <large> <small>.

Use various attributes of the <P> tag to change font size, colour and alignment of text.

Be able to use subscripts and superscripts.

Add horizontal rulers

insert special characters.

Lists

Create different types of list – unordered lists, ordered lists, definition lists.

Create a list that is nested inside another list

Links

Be able to add different types of link in your web pages. These should include links to other HTML documents, either offline or on the web.

They could also include other documents such as WORD and PDF, as well as email links.

Add code that will determine the colour of links depending on whether visited or clicked on.

Web graphics

Understand the characteristics of graphics file formats used on the Web.

Add images to web pages using <IMG> tag. Be able to size images and include the ALT attribute appropriately.

Be able to align text around a picture and add background colour or a background image to your web pages.

Include an image map with hot spots that can be clicked on.

Chapter 6 (week 6)

Creating web pages with HTML

6.1 The World-Wide-Web

As previously stated, the World Wide Web is a linked collection of documents stored on the Internet, that allow people to communicate ideas with millions of people right across the World. In this section we will be looking at the development of the World Wide Web and also looking at the importance of it today.

6.1.1 A short history of the World Wide Web

There are many places where you can find out about the development of the World Wide Web. Many books on the Internet, and creating web sites or web pages include a section that summarizes the development. There are possibly thousands of web sites that are devoted to this topic. The most authoritative account is to be found in the book "Weaving the Web", as this is written by the inventor.

I intend to summarize the events leading to the earlier development of the World Wide Web, by creating a chronological listing of important events. I leave it to the reader to fill in the gaps by reading up material on the web or from a number of books that contain this information.

1980s

Tim Berners-Lee whilst working at CERN in Switzerland built a personal database of people and software media. He called this Enquire. This database contained hypertext so that he could include links to material in other documents.

1989

Tim Berners-Lee wrote a proposal for Managing Information over the Internet. In it he suggested that information could be transferred over the Internet using hypertext.

1990

Tim Berners-Lee built all the necessary tools for a working web site. He created the Hypertext Transfer Protocol (HTTP), Hypertext Markup Language (HTML) and the first web browser called World Wide Web. This web browser also included a built-in editor. He also created the first HTTP server software called CERN httpd.

1991

Servers appeared in other institutions within Europe.

1992

There are 26 web servers in the world.

1993

There are over 200 web servers in the world and CERN announced that the World Wide Web would be free to everyone. In this year NCSA (National Center for Supercomputing Applications) at the University of Illinois released the first version of Mosaic – a web browser that made it possible for people using PCs and Apple Macs to access the World Wide Web.

1994

The World Wide Web Consortium (W3C) was set up to develop Internet protocols and standards for the World Wide Web. Netscape brought out Netscape Navigator.

1996 – 1998

In this period the World Wide Web started to become commercialized as many more people started to trade on the Internet. Microsoft bundles Internet Explorer with the Windows 95. By 1998 Internet Explorer has a third of the browser market.

1999 – 2001

The low interest rates of this period encouraged people to speculate in new start-up ventures that involved the Internet. These were often referred to as dot com (.com) companies. Many of these made their founders millionaires overnight. Many other dot com ventures crashed spectacularly as they were greatly overvalued and could not realise what they promised.

2002 - present

Investment continues to pour into the Internet and World Wide Web. Telecommunication companies increase the bandwidth for Internet traffic and also make Internet Access much cheaper so that most people can afford it. In this period it became apparent that for most people the Internet and World Wide Web was becoming an important part of their life. It no longer was just a source of information for their studies or research, but also became much more significant for entertainment and shopping.

6.1.2   The importance of the Wide World Web

The World Wide Web is most important as it allows you to use the Internet easily at the click of a mouse. If you did not have the World Wide Web, accessing the Internet would be much more difficult. Imagine having to use FTP at a command prompt, having to log on to a particular computer, then use FTP commands to list the files before being able to specify which ones you wish to transfer.

Nowadays, browsing the World Wide Web is the most popular application on a personal computer. It is sufficient to think about how you use the computer in everyday life to appreciate how important the World Wide Web is.

If you are a student, you probably justify your time on the Internet by stating that it is very useful for finding relevant information for your current project. You typically start by entering some keywords into a search engine. This will list many links relating to the keywords entered. Then when you click on these links the associated HTML documents etc are transferred to your computer. Research in this manner is very easy, possibly much easier than going to a library and taking out some books – assuming of course that the library has the books you want.

The Internet and World Wide Web are typically used in many other different ways. It is used to keep in contact with friends and acquaintances. Most people use email in place of writing letters. This has the advantage that it is quicker and cheaper than post. You can also keep up-to-date with friends using social networking sites such as facebook. This provides facilities to post pictures and messages on the site, as well as being able to send messages.

If you want a more interactive means of communication you can use some form of internet chat, or you can use skype on your computer in place of using a telephone. If you use facebook you already have a facility to chat with friends logged onto facebook.

The Internet and World Wide Web has also changed the way we shop. The introduction of online shopping companies such as Amazon mean that most people buy books online, rather than go to a book shop. There is a very good reason for this, there is much more choice, as they can list a much greater quantity of books than any book shop can hope to stock. Also, because Amazon has lower overheads and deals with larger quantities, there are many occasions when the books are discounted. There are now online stores for just about any product that could previously be bought in a shop. Online shopping is now considered to be relatively safe with the introduction of paypal.

It is also now much easier for people to sell their own goods without having to have their own web site. The main example that comes to mind is ebay. But it is also, possibly even easier to sell your unwanted books and other products on Amazon.

6.2 Software for creating web pages

We will now be looking at how you can create web pages.

There are three main ways that someone could adopt to create web pages:

1. Use a text editor such as **notepad** and type in the text and HTML manually

2. Use an HTML editor to enter the document including HTML coding. An HTML editor provides help with the HTML.

3. Use a WYSIWYG package such as **Microsoft Frontpage** which does most of it for you.

Whatever method is used, you need to use a web-browser to view the completed web page.

In this book we will be concentrating on method 1. So we will only need to have access to an editor (notepad) and a browser (Microsoft Internet Explorer or Mozilla Firefox). The reason I have chosen to do this is that it is the best way to learn about HTML. Some people prefer to use products such as Microsoft FrontPage because it requires little knowledge of HTML and that it is quicker to complete a finished document.

You are already familiar with what is meant by web page and HTML documents, as these concepts have already been covered by your previous introduction to the Internet.

We will start this session by making ourselves more familiar with what an HTML document looks like. This can be achieved by downloading a web page, and examining the source code.

6.3 Examining the source code of a web page

The picture below illustrates how the Knockhardy Science notes site appears using Mozilla Firefox. To obtain the source code, click on **Page Source** from within the **View** pop-down menu.

Once you have done this you should end up with something like this:

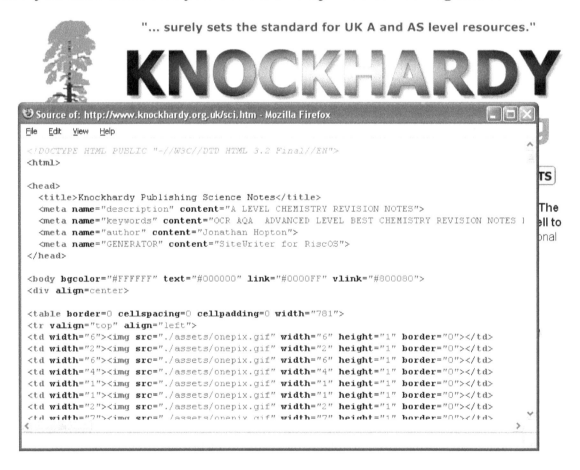

The code appears in a new window. You will notice that keywords and filenames are colour-coded, if you are using Mozilla Firefox. Because the source code is opened by the browser, you are not able to edit the source code. You can however save the source code, print it, and do a number of other things – as long as you don't modify it in any way.

If you use Microsoft Internet Explorer as your browser, you obtain the following:

Clicking on the option **Source** from within the pop-down menu **View**, will open up another window with the source code in it. In this case the web page is opened with notepad.

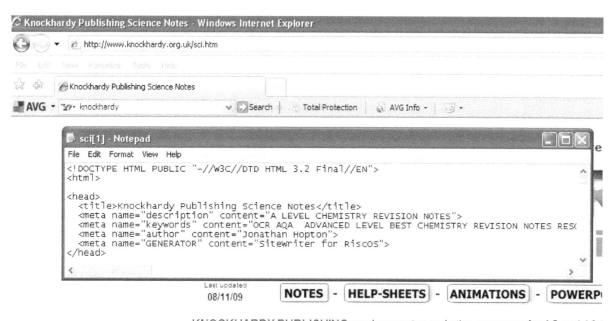

Because the source code is opened using an editor rather than a browser, you can also edit the source code. It is for this reason, that we will use Internet Explorer to develop web pages.

Exercise 6-1

1. Copy and fill in the blanks for the following text about the World Wide Web.

The concept of the _____ was invented by Tim Berners-Lee in 1990. He created the _____ protocol to specify how data stored on _____ can be transferred between different computers logged on to the _____. The also created the first _____ to read web pages. These web pages were coded using a language called _____ and included special links to other web pages called _____.

2. The Knockhardy Science notes site contains very useful notes for A-level chemistry.

(a) Locate and download this page from the Internet

(b) Save the document, and some of the included pictures into a folder in your user area. List properties of this file – including file type and size.

(c) Obtain a listing of the source code using the method suggested above. Try modifying some of the source code and save the modifications. Close the html document and then open it again to view the changes.

(d) Open the document using notepad, so that you can edit the source code.

(e) Convert the document to word format so that you can edit the format of the text, without having to worry about HTML.

(f) Use the Internet to find free notes about HTML. Write down the URL of at least 3 locations where useful HTML notes can be found.

(g) Check out the latest specification for HTML at the site:

www.w3.org/TR/WD-html40

6.4   Creating an HTML document.

An HTML document is merely a text document that is saved with the file extension **.html** or **.htm**. Normally HTML documents have embedded commands or tags to format the document.

You can create a variety of objects by right-clicking your mouse, and then select new.

On my computer I am able to choose **Text document**. If you click on this you obtain a new text document.

The alternative to doing this is to create a shortcut for notepad. You can then double-click on the shortcut every time you want to create a text document.

Either way, you will obtain this.

If you double-click on this icon, you get taken into notepad.

To turn this text document into an html file, you need to save the file with file extension **.html**.

You also need to click on the pop-down menu for **Save as Type**, and change it to **All files**.

Now that you have done this you can start entering the text for your first html document.

Once saved the icon for the HTML document will look like this. This can be easily be renamed.

To start editing the new HTML document just double-click the icon. If you have not entered any text, the contents of the window will be empty. To edit this you need to select the **View** pop-down menu, then click on **Source**. You need to do this each time you edit your code.

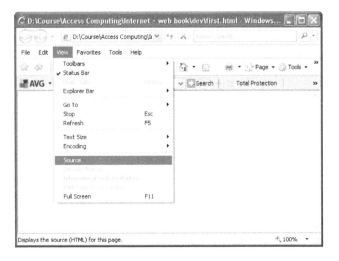

Clicking on **Source**, opens a new window that can be used to edit the html file using notepad. In this example some text with html tags to format it have been typed in.

You then click on **Save** – within the **File** pop-down menu, each time you have made changes and need to save them.

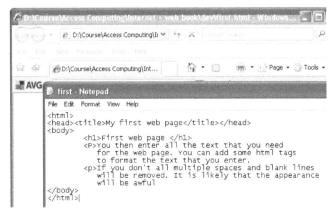

If you click on the refresh button, or if you close the file and click on the icon for the HTML file, you obtain this. You will notice that the words "First web page" are larger and in bold. Also that the text has been arranged in two paragraphs.

6.5   A first look at HTML

The following text document was created using **notepad** and saved as Aesop.html. It is an appropriate fable as it reminds me of many students I have taught in the past.

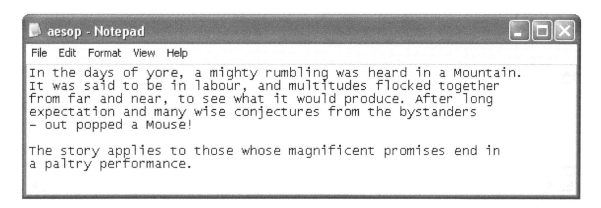

The file Aesop.html should have an icon that corresponds to an HTML document, even though it contains only normal text. When you click on the icon, you should be able to view the text using the default browser (Microsoft Internet Explorer).

The text will be formatted as follows when you view it with Microsoft Internet Explorer.

You will notice that many of the features of the original document have disappeared. The most obvious changes are that all blank lines and multiple spaces have been removed. Also the text font is different.

The result produced here is obviously unacceptable, so it is now time to start using some basic HTML commands.

The following shows the same text file with some embedded HTML tags.

<u>Example 1</u>

```
<html>
<head>
     <title>Aesop fable 10</title>
</head>
<body>
<H1>The Mountain in Labour</H1>
<BR>Fable 10
<P>
     In the days of yore, a mighty rumbling was heard in a
     Mountain. It was said to be in labour, and multitudes
     flocked together from far and near, to see what it would
     produce. After long expectation and many wise conjectures
     from the bystanders - out popped a Mouse!
<P>
     The story applies to those whose magnificent promises end
     in a paltry performance.
</body>
</html>
```

The following illustrates how Internet Explorer formats the text.

Title bar

Notes:

1. A web page should always begin with <html> and end with </html>

2. There are often two parts to an HTML file. The head is just used for a few things – in this case to specify the title. The body contains the bulk of all text and HTML code.

3. The head of an HTML document appears between <HEAD> and </HEAD>

4. The body of an HTML document appears between <BODY> and </BODY>

5. One of the things that we can insert within the head is a title. Text between <title> and </title> appear on the title bar of the browser.

6. There are 6 header types. H1 is the largest. Any text between <H1> and </H1> will be considered to be a size 1 header, and have a corresponding large font. The smallest size header is H6.

7. The <BR> tag is used to create a new line. Text after this appears on a new line.

8. The tag <P> is used to start a new paragraph.

6.6   Summary of some basic HTML tags used so far

<HTML> ... </HTML>   This is used to enclose the entire HTML document

<HEAD> ... </HEAD>   This is used to enclose the head of the HTML document

<TITLE> ... </TITLE>   This indicates the title – which appears in the title bar of the browser

<BODY> ... </BODY>   This is used to enclose the body of the HTML document.

<P> ... </P> Start of a new paragraph. Don't need to use </P> to specify the end of a paragraph.

 ... </BR>   A line break, or new-line.

<H1> ... </H1>   Heading size 1 (largest)

<H2> ... </H2>   Heading size 2.

<H3> ... </H3>   Heading size 3.

<H4> ... </H4>   Heading size 4.

<H5> ... </H5>   Heading size 5

<H6> ... </H6>   Heading size 6 (smallest)

6.7　Bold, underline and italic

Most people who use Microsoft Word are use to using bold, underline and italics. To do this in your html documents, you need to be able to use the tags <B>, <U> and <I>

Example 2

```
<html>
<head><title>Bold, underline and italic</title><head>
<body>
    This demonstrates the tags B, U and I
    <P><B> This text is bold</B>
    <P><U> and this text is underlined</U>
    <P><I> and this text is in italic</I>
    <P><B><U><I>Finally, this text uses all 3 tags
        </I></U></B>
</body>
</html>
```

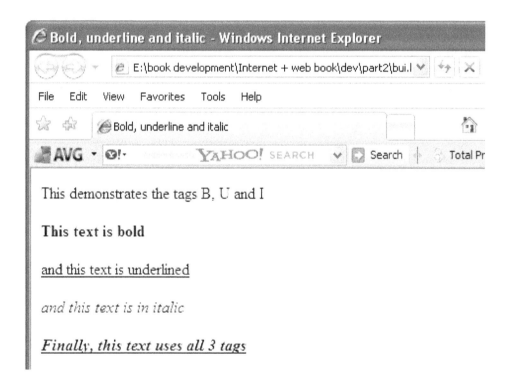

Notes:

1. When you use the <B> tag to make your text bold, you must remember to use </B> when you want to return to normal text.

2. The same rule applies for underlined and italic text. That is, these should be terminated with </U> and </I> respectively.

6.8   More about paragraphs and fonts

In the following example Aesop.html has been modified so that the main text is centred, blue, and size 4 using the Helvetica font.

Example 3

```
<HTML>
<HEAD>
<TITLE>Aesop fable 10</TITLE>
</HEAD>
<BODY>
<H1>THE MOUNTAIN IN LABOUR</H1>
<BR>FABLE 10
<P>
<FONT SIZE = "4", COLOR = "Blue ", FACE = "helvetica">
<CENTER>
      In the days of yore, a mighty rumbling was heard in a
      Mountain. It was said to be in labour, and multitudes
      flocked together from far and near, to see what it would
      produce. After long expectation and many wise conjectures
      from the bystanders - out popped a Mouse!
<P>
      The story applies to those whose magnificent promises end
      in a paltry performance.
</CENTER>
</FONT>
</BODY>
</HTML>
```

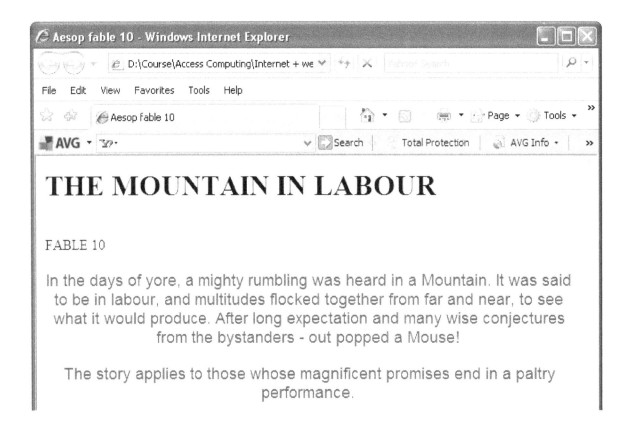

98

Notes:

1. The browser window in this example has been resized. The text is wrapped accordingly.

2. The text is centred, size 4, blue and with the Helvetica font.

3. The tag <center> is used to place the text on each line at the centre of the window. Notice the American spelling – you have to spell it this way.

4. An alternative to using the <center> tag is to add an attribute for each paragraph when you use the <P> tag. That is use the following:

   <P align = center>   … </P> in place of ….

5. Likewise you can align text left or right using align = left etc.

6. You can add other attributes to the <P> tag, such as font size etc.

6.9   Using the <pre> tag

The <pre> tag is used for preformatted text. That is you want the text to appear exactly the way you enter it.

Example 4

```
<html>
<head><title>Use of pre tag</title></head>
<body>
    Program listing follows:
    <P>
    <pre>

    #include <iostream>
    using namespace std;

    int main()
    {

        cout << "n\t\tterm" << endl;
        int n = 1;
        while (n <= 10)
        {
            cout << n << "\t\t" << (1.0 / n) << endl;
            n++;
        }
        return 0;
    }

    </pre>
</body>
</html>
```

Display program listing using <pre> tag

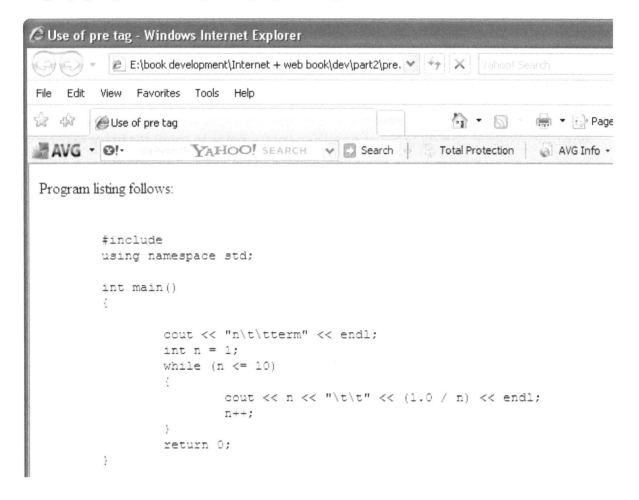

Notes

1. In this case program source code is displayed. Pre is usually used in those situations where text is formatted, and you want to preserve this format.

6.10   Use of subscripts and superscripts

The following example demonstrates the use of subscripts and superscripts.

Example 5

```
<HTML>
<HEAD>
<TITLE>Chemical equation</TITLE>
</HEAD>
<BODY>
      Reduction of Chromate 6
      <P>
      Cr<SUB>2</SUB>O<SUB>7</SUB><SUP>2-</SUP> + 14H<SUP>
      +</SUP> + 6e -> 2Cr<SUP>3+</SUP> + 7H<SUB>2</SUB>O
</BODY>
</HTML>
```

Produces the following output:

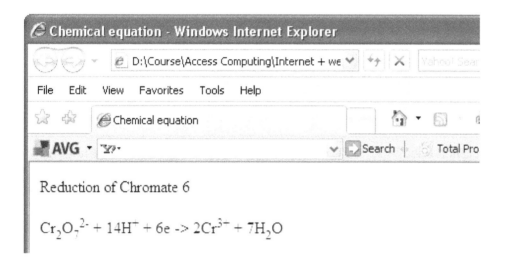

Notes:

1. Text between ^{and} is raised. That is it becomes superscript.

2. Text between _{and} is lowered. That is it becomes subscript.

3. This example also demonstrates the use of indentation. This is not essential, but does make the document more readable

6.11   Summary of additional HTML tags

\<I> ... \</I>	Italic text
\<B> ... \</B>	Bold text
\<U> ... \</U>	Underlined text
\<CENTER> ... \</CENTRE>	Centred text
\^{... \}	Superscript
_{... \}	Subscript
\<FONT SIZE = "4"> ... \</FONT>	Set font size to 4
\<FONT SIZE = +1> ... \</FONT>	Increase current font size by 1
\<FONT SIZE = -1> ... \</FONT>	Decrease current font size by 1
\<FONT COLOR = "RED"> ... \</FONT>	Change to red font
\<FONT COLOR = #FF0000> ... \</FONT>	Change to red font
\<FONT FACE = "ariel"> ... \</FONT>	Display text using ariel font.
\<FONT FACE = "ariel, helvetica"> ... \</FONT>	Display text using ariel, and if not available use helvetica.
\<P align = right> ... \</P>	Left align the paragraph
\<P align = center> ... \</P>	Centre align the paragraph
\<P align = left> ... \</P>	Left align the paragraph

Common colour values

Red	FF0000
Green	00FF00
Blue	0000FF
Yellow	FFFF00
Orange	FFA500
Gold	FFD700
Beige	F5F5DC
Gray	808080
Navy	000080
Black	000000
White	FFFFFF

6.12 Special characters

Any other characters that are not on the keyboard are usually referred to as special characters.

Example 6

```
<HTML>
<HEAD>
<TITLE>Special characters</TITLE>
</HEAD>
<BODY>
      &#169; Tony Hawken 2002
      <BR>
      &frac34; pound of grapes
</BODY>
</HTML>
```

Notes:

1. All special characters start with an ampersand (&).

2. The special character can be specified with # followed by a number. For example `&#169` is used for the copy right symbol ©.

3. Alternatively it can be specified with a keyword. For example `&frac34` is used to specify the fraction ¾.

Table of some commonly used special characters

Character	numeric code	code name	description
"	"	"	Quotation mark
&	&	&	ampersand
©	©	©	copyright
®	®	®	Registed trademark
±	&#177	±	Plus or minus
¼	¼	¼	One quarter
½	½	½	One half
¾	¾	¾	Three quarters
Æ	Æ	&Aelig;	Capital AE ligature
æ	æ	æ	Small ae ligature
é	é	&eacute	Small acute e
×	×		multiply
÷	÷		divide

6.13   Adding rulers

The following examples demonstrate the inclusion of horizontal rulers. A horizontal ruler is merely a horizontal straight line. They are a simple way of splitting up a web page and making it more presentable

Example 7

```
<HTML>
<HEAD>
<TITLE>ruler</TITLE>
</HEAD>
<BODY>
     <P> green ruler, size 10, 70 %
     <HR SIZE = 10 WIDTH = 70% COLOR = "green">
     <P> blue ruler, size 5, 100%
     <HR SIZE = 5 WIDTH = 100% COLOR = "blue">
</BODY>
</HTML>
```

Notes

1. A horizontal ruler is created with the tag <HR>.

2. If you don't mention the width it will span the width of the web page.

3. The width of a horizontal ruler is normally expressed as a percentage of the width of the web page.

4. The size of a horizontal ruler determines how thick the line is.

5. You can determine the colour by using the COLOR attribute.

Example 8

```
<HTML>
<HEAD>
<TITLE>ruler2</TITLE>
</HEAD>
<BODY>
     <P> black ruler, Size 2, 50%, left alignment
     <HR SIZE = 2 WIDTH = 50% COLOR = "black" ALIGN = "left">
     <P> brown ruler, size 2, 50%, right alignment
     <HR SIZE = 2 WIDTH = 50% COLOR = "brown" ALIGN = "right">
</BODY>
</HTML>
```

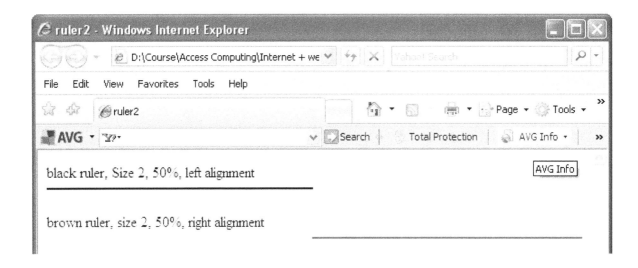

Notes

1. This example demonstrates that you can position the line on a web page using the ALIGN attribute. You can choose from left, right and center.

Exercise 6-2

1. The HTML text required to display the following:

   These are the people:
   Tony
   John

   is

   (a) These are the people: <P> Tony <P> John

   (b) These are the people:
       Tony
       John

   (c) These are the people:
 Tony
 John

2. Give HTML commands to achieve the following:

   (i) Put the following text in bold typeface: "I am bold"

   (ii) Put the following text in italic typeface: "This is italic"

   (iii)   Create a level 1 header: "I'm a header"

3. Reproduce the following in HTML. The horizontal rulers should span 50%
   of the width of the web page and should be blue.

   Mathematical expressions

   ───────────────────────────────

   $\log_a N^x = x \log_a N$

   ───────────────────────────────

   $\frac{1}{2} + \frac{1}{4} = \frac{3}{4}$

   ───────────────────────────────

Chapter 7 (week 7)

Lists and Links

7.1   introduction to lists

The following demonstrates the creation of a simple list using the <BR> tag.

Example 9

```
<html>
<title>Winnie-the-Pooh</title>
<body>
<H4>Contents</H4><p>
<BR>In which we are introduced to Winnie-the-Pooh and some
     Bees, and the story begins
<BR>In which Pooh goes visiting and gets into a tight place
<BR>In which Pooh and Piglet go hunting and nearly catch a
     Woozle
<BR>In which Piglet meets a Heffalump
<BR>In which Eeyore has a birthday and gets two presents
<BR>In which Kanga and Baby Roo come to the Forest, and Piglet
     has a bath
<BR>In which Christopher Robin leads an expedition to the
     North Pole
<BR>In which Piglet is entirely surrounded by water
<BR>In which Christopher Robin gives a Pooh Party, and we say
     good-bye
</body>
```

7.2 Unordered lists

An unordered list is the simplest type of list. Each list element is preceded by a bullet point.

<u>Example 10</u>

```
<html>
<title>Winnie-the-Pooh</title>
<body>
<H4>Contents</H4><p>
<UL>
      <LI>In which we are introduced to Winnie-the-Pooh and
          some Bees, and the story begins
      <LI>In which Pooh goes visiting and gets into a tight
          place
      <LI>In which Pooh and Piglet go hunting and nearly catch
          a Woozle
      <LI>In which Piglet meets a Heffalump
      <LI>In which Eeyore has a birthday and gets two presents
      <LI>In which Kanga and Baby Roo come to the Forest, and
          Piglet has a bath
      <LI>In which Christopher Robin leads an expedition to the
          North Pole
      <LI>In which Piglet is entirely surrounded by water
      <LI>In which Christopher Robin gives a Pooh Party, and we
          say good-bye
</UL>
</body>
```

An unordered list

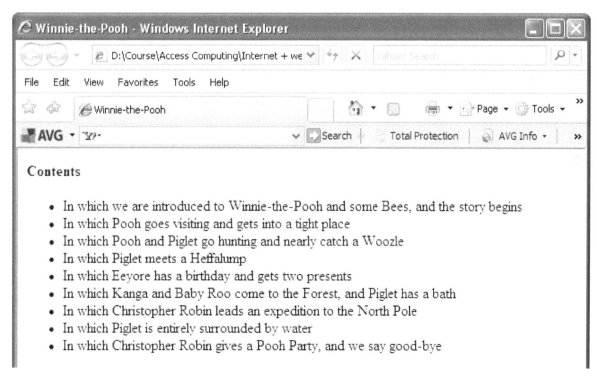

Notes

1. An unordered list starts with the tag <UL> and ends with the tag </UL>

2. Each item in the list begins with the tag <LI>. You can terminate each list item with the tag </LI>, but you don't have to, this is optional.

3. Each list item is preceded by a bullet point. You can specify the type of bullet point required.

7.3   Ordered Lists

An ordered list is very similar to that of an unordered list. This time each list element is preceded by a number. The numbers are generated automatically starting with 1 by default.

Example 11

```
<HTML>
<HEAD>
<TITLE>Winnie-the-Pooh</TITLE>
<BODY>
<H4>Contents</H4>
<P>
<OL>
   <LI>In which we are introduced to Winnie-the-Pooh and some
      Bees, and the story begins
   <LI>In which Pooh goes visiting and gets into a tight place
   <LI>In which Pooh and Piglet go hunting and nearly catch a
      Woozle
   <LI>In which Piglet meets a Heffalump
   <LI>In which Eeyore has a birthday and gets two presents
   <LI>In which Kanga and Baby Roo come to the Forest, and
      Piglet has a bath
   <LI>In which Christopher Robin leads an expedition to the
      North Pole
   <LI>In which Piglet is entirely surrounded by water
   <LI>In which Christopher Robin gives a Pooh Party, and we
      say good-bye
</OL>
</BODY>
</HTML>
```

An ordered list

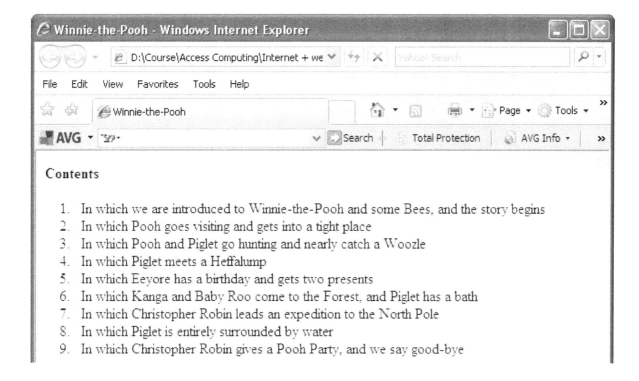

Notes

1. Each ordered list begins with the tag <OL> and ends with </OL>

2. Each item in the list starts with the tag <LI>

7.4 Definition Lists

Definition lists are indented lists without using numbers or symbols. They are typically used in glossaries or in any situation where you have a pairing of a word or phrase and the definition of that word or phrase.

Example 12

```
<HTML>
<body>
<H1>Further Normalization</H1>
<DL><DT>First Normal Form
    <DD>A relation is in first normal form (1NF) iff it
        contains atomic values only
    <DT>Second Normal Form
    <DD>A relation is in second normal form (2NF) iff it is in
        1NF and every non-key attribute is fully dependant on
        the entire primary key. That is there are no
        functional dependencies that involve only part of the
        primary key.
    <DT>Third Normal Form
    <DD>A relation is in third normal form (3NF) iff it is in
        2NF and all non-key attributes are mutually
        independent. That is, there are no functional
        dependencies where the determinant is a non-key
        attribute.
</DL>
</body>
</html>
```

A definition list

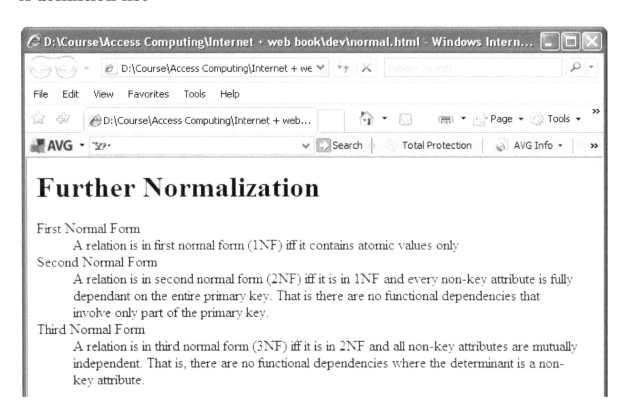

Notes:

1. A definition list starts with the tag <DL>

2. The tag <DT> is used before the term being defined

3. The tag <DD> is used before the definition for the term

4. All of these tags can be optionally closed using </DL>, </DT> and </DD>. In this example the optional closing tags were not used.

7.5   Nested Lists

A nested list can be created, by creating a list inside a list. Note how in this example the lists are indented. It is vital to do this to ensure that each list is properly terminated.

Example 13

```
<html>
<body>
<OL>
    <LI> Simplify these algebraic expressions
    <OL type = "a">
        <LI> a + a + a
        <LI> 3b + 2b - b
        <LI> c + c + 3c
    </OL>
    <LI> Find the next two terms in the following sequences
    <OL type = "i">
        <LI> 11, 13, 15, 17, 19, ......
        <LI> 100, 89, 78, 67, 56, ......
        <LI> 4, 11, 18, 25, 32, ......
        <LI> 50, 45, 40, 35, 30, ......
    </OL>
</OL>
</body>
</html>
```

Nested lists – a pair of ordered lists inside an ordered list

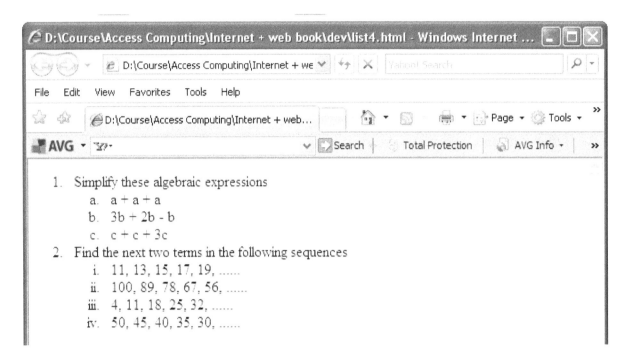

Notes:

1. This example shows an ordered list with two ordered lists inserted in it.

2. The type attribute is used to change the format of numbering. A type value of "a", gives lowercase letters. A type-value "i", gives lower-case Roman numerals.

3. You can also use a type value = "A" for Capital letters and "I" for capital Roman numbers.

4. You can also insert an unordered list in an ordered list and vis versa.

Exercise 7-1

1. Give HTML code fragments that create the following lists:

   (a) An unordered list containing 2 items (Bread, butter)
   (b) An ordered list that contains 3 items (Mathematics, Physics, Chemistry).

2. Rewrite these ingredients as an unordered list, and with an appropriate heading:

   Cream of Leak soup

   2 large leeks
   1 small potato
   1 medium sized carrot
   1oz of butter or margarine
   2 pints of vegetable stock
   Salt & pepper to taste
   ¼ pint of fresh double cream

3. Modify your web page for question 2. This time create an ordered list with lower-case Roman numerals.

4. In this question you are to create a glossary for the following terms:

   Internet, www, web browser, web server, HTML, hypertext

   (a) Create this glossary using an appropriate definition list.

   (b) Add an appropriate heading above the glossary.

7.6   linking to documents on the web

This first example illustrates how to link to different types of documents on the web.

Example 14

```
<html>
<head><title>Links to resources on the web</title></head>
<body>
    <H1>Resources on the Internet</H1>
    <P> The following demonstrate how you can create links to
        resources on the Internet
    <P>
       W3c HTML 5 draft
       <A href = "http://www.w3.org/TR/html5/">Link 1</A>
    <P>
       Barebones html notes
       <A href = "http://werbach.com/barebones/notes.html">Link 2
       </A>
    <P>
       Core web programming notes (Forms)
       <A href = "http://notes.corewebprogramming.com/student/
       Servers-and-Forms.pdf">Link 3</A>
    <P>
       Converting PowerPoint Presentations to HTML
       <A href = "http://www.ferris.edu/tac/docs/
       PowerPoint_to_HTML.doc">Link 4</A>
</body>
</html>
```

Links to resources on the Internet

Resources on the Internet

The following demonstrate how you can create links to resources on the Internet

W3c HTML 5 draft Link 1

Barebones html notes Link 2

Core web programming notes (Forms) Link 3

Converting PowerPoint Presentations to HTML Link 4

Notes

1. A hypertext link always starts with the tag A.

2. The key-word href associates the URL of the object that you wish to link to.

3. The text between <A href = " "> and </A> determines what you click on click on. By default this text will be underlined.

4. The first link is to a directory or folder. Usually there is a file called index.html in this directory that is used.

5. The second link is to an html file on the Internet.

6. The third and fourth links are to a PDF and a WORD file.

7. You can create a link to any object for which you can write a URL.

There are many types of files that are available on the Internet that you can link to. The following selection of file formats is commonly used.

Description document	extension	Software required to read the
Hypertext mark-up language	.html	Microsoft Internet Explorer or Mozilla Firefox
Text	.txt	notepad or similar text editor
Portable document format	.pdf	Acrobat reader
Word document	.doc	Microsoft Word
Postscript	.ps	Aladdin ghostscript or similar postscript viewer.
TEX	.tex or .dvi	TEX or LATEX
PowerPoint	.ppt	Microsoft PowerPoint or PowerPoint-reader
ZIP archive	.zip	WINZIP or ZipCentral etc

7.7　Linking to your own web pages

When you are creating your own web pages, most of the time, you will want to link pages that you have created. In the example illustrated below 3 HTML files have been created - page1.html is in the same folder as homepage.html. The other, page2.html is in a folder called page2folder.

Example 15

```
<html>
<head><title>Homepage</title></head>
<body>
    <OL>
     <LI>Link to page1 (found in current folder)
         <A href = "page1.html">Page1</A>
     <LI>Link to Page 2 (found in folder page2folder)
         <A href = "page2folder/page2.html">page2</A>
    </OL>
</body>
</html>
```

Notes

1. If the html file is in the same folder, you just need to name the file itself.

2. If the html file is in a subfolder, you can name the subfolder relatively. So the reference page2folder/page2.html, refers to a file called page2.html that is in a folder called page2folder, and that this folder is within the current folder.

3. You can name a folder using absolute addressing. Imagine that the file called homepage.html is on the C: drive and that your working folder is called webwork. You can then refer to hompage.html as

    c:/webwork/homepage.html

and page2.html as

    c:/webwork/page2folder/page2.html.

7.8   Linking to a specific part of a web page.

As web pages get larger it is necessary to be able to link to a part of the same page or even a specific location on another web page. This makes it much easier for a user to find things and avoids the need to scroll down a page to look for a certain item.

To be able to do this you need to identify a location in a given web page. This is achieved by inserting an anchor point, where you name that part of the page.

Once this has been done you can create a link to that anchor point. If you click on the corresponding link, the web page will scroll up or down to that particular location. You can also refer to anchor points in other HTML documents.

Example 16

```
<html>
<head><title>Link to a different part of the page
</title><head>
<body>
    <A name = "begin">
    <H3>Beginning of text</H3>
    You can click here to go to the end
    <A href = "#end">end</A>
    This is a small demonstration on how to use anchor
    points, so that you can link to them from within this
    page, or in fact from some other page. Normally you would
    only do this if the web page is much bigger so that you
    need to scroll down the page to read all of the content.
    <P>
    This section shows how you can click to a specific part
    of another HTML file.
    <P>
    Click on here to get contact details
    <A href = "page2.html/#contact">Contact me</A>
    <P>
    <A name = "end">
    <H3>End of text</H3>
    You can click on this link to go to the beginning
    <A href = "#begin">beginning</A>
</body>
</html>
```

Web page with anchor points and links to them

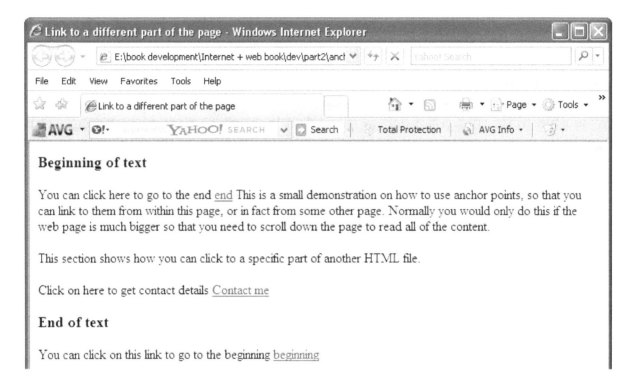

Notes

1. The code **<A name = "begin">** creates an anchor point at that position in the document. That is, this position in the document is called **end**.

2. The code **<A href = "#end">end</A>** creates a link to the anchor point called end. Notice that you need to refer to this anchor point as **#end**.

3. The code **<A href = "page2.html/#contact">Contact me</A>** demonstrates that you can link to an anchor point in a different HTML document, in this case **page2.html**.

7.9 Email links

The example that follows shows how you can link to an email address using the mailto protocol. Most browsers support mailto – certainly Microsoft Internet Explorer and Mozilla Firefox.

Example 17

```
<html>
<head><title>Send email</title></head>
<body>
    You can contact me by email using the following link
    <A href = "mailto:tony_hawken@talktalk.net">Email Tony
Hawken</A>
</body>
</html>
```

Notes

1. The URL associated with href is prefixed with mailto:. This identifies that what follows is an email address.

2. Clicking on the link will open your default mail client. In my case this is Microsoft Outlook Express.

Exercise 7-2

1. Write HTML code to achieve the following:

    (a) Create an HTML document called links.html. This document should include a large heading "HTML resources", and a paragraph about HTML.

    (b) Write HTML code to create a link to the site http://www.w3.org and text to indicate that this is the World Wide Web Consortium (w3c).

    (c) Search the web for a useful PDF file that contains information about HTML. Include a link to this and include appropriate information to indicate what the resource is.

    (d) Create a mailto link, so that someone can contact you by email.

    (e) Create an anchor point at the top of this page. Call it top.

    (f) Create a link at the bottom of the web page to the anchor point called top.

Chapter 8 (week 8)

Web graphics

8.1   Use of simple graphics in a web page

Simple graphic images - typically in GIF or JPG format, can easily be included in an HTML document by using the <IMG> tag as illustrated below.

<u>Example 18</u>

```
<html>
<head>
    <title>Kenyan flag</title>
</head>
<body>
    <H1>Kenyan flag</H1>
    <P>The Kenyan flag displayed here is stored in GIF
        format. GIF is a very popular file format for graphics
        on the internet  because of the small amount of
        storage required.
    </P>
    <img src="Kenya_flag_11182.gif" width = 100 height = 75
        alt = "Kenyan flag">
</body>
</html>
```

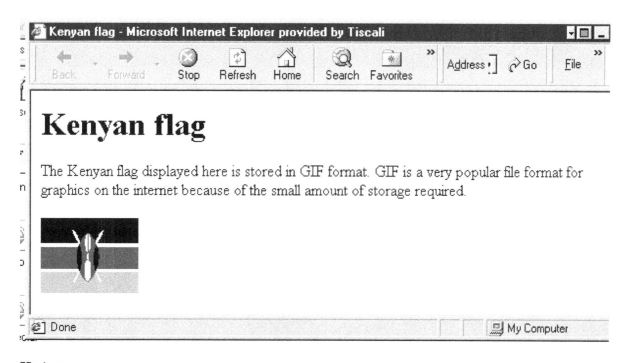

Notes:

1. The **src** attribute is used to name the file containing the graphic image.

2. The **height** and **width** attributes specify the size of the displayed image in pixels.

3. Unless you specify otherwise the image will appear at the bottom left of the window

4. The **alt** attribute should always be used to tell a user what an image is - just in case they have graphics switched off for their browser, or the image specified cannot be found.

8.2 Alignment of text around a picture

Example 19

```
<html>
<head>
    <title>Kenyan flag</title>
</head>
<body>
    <H1>Kenyan flag</H1>
    <P>The Kenyan flag displayed here is stored in GIF
        format. GIF is a very popular file format for graphics
        on the internet because of the small amount of storage
        required.
    </P>
    <img src="Kenya_flag_11182.gif" width = 100 height = 75>
    Some additional text has now been added. You would expect
    This text text to appear below the flag. This usually is
    not the case - instead the text will fill the space to
    the right of the picture on the bottom line of the flag.
</body>
</html>
```

Kenyan flag

The Kenyan flag displayed here is stored in GIF format. GIF is a very popular file format for graphics on the internet because of the small amount of storage required.

Some additional text has now been added. You would expect this text text to appear below the flag. This usually is not the case - instead the text will fill the space to the right of the picture.

Notes:

1. We could have placed the last section of text completely underneath the flag. This could be achieved using a <P> paragraph tag.

2. Alternatively we can if we choose ensure that the text surrounds the picture.

3. We can also align the picture, as you will see in the next example.

8.3   Vertical and horizontal alignment

Example 20

```
<html>
<head>
<title>Kenyan flag</title>
</head>
<body>
    <H1>Kenyan flag</H1>
    The Kenyan flag displayed here is stored in GIF format.
    GIF is a very popular file format for graphics on the
    internet because of the small amount of storage required.
    In this example I have removed all paragraph tags so that
    the picture floats within the text.
    <img src="Kenya_flag_11182.gif" width = 100 height = 75
        align = "bottom" align = "right"
        alt = "Kenyan flag - GIF file">
    Some additional text has now been added. You would expect
    this text to appear below the flag. This usually is not
    the case -  instead the text will fill the space to the
    right of the picture on the bottom line of the flag
    unless attributes have been used to specify where the
    image is place in relation to the text.
</body>
</html>
```

Kenyan flag

The Kenyan flag displayed here is stored in GIF format. GIF is a very popular file format for graphics on the internet because of the small amount of storage required. In this example I have removed all paragraph tags so that the picture floats within the text. Some additional text has now been added. You would expect this text text to appear below the flag. This usually is not the case - instead the text will fill the space to the right of the picture on the bottom line of the flag unless attributes have been used to specify where the image is place in relation to the text.

Notes:

1. The attributes **top**, **middle**, **bottom**, **absmiddle**, **absbottom** are used to align a picture relative to some text

2. To align the bottom of an image with the bottom of the text use **align = "bottom"**

3. A picture can be placed to the left or right of some text using the **left** or **right** attributes with **align**.

8.4 Stopping text wrap

Example 21

```
<html>
<head>
    <title>Kenyan flag</title>
</head>
<body>
    <H1>Kenyan flag</H1>
        The Kenyan flag displayed here is stored in GIF
        format. GIF is a very popular file format for graphics
        on the internet because of the small amount of storage
        required.
    <img src="Kenya_flag_11182.gif" width = 100 height = 75
        Align=left>
    <BR CLEAR=right>
    Some additional text has now been added. You would expect
    this text text to appear below the flag. This usually is
    not the case - instead the text will fill the space to
    the right of the picture on the bottom line of the flag.
</body>
</html>
```

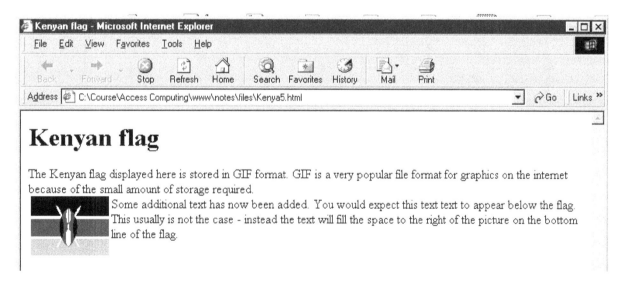

Notes:

1. <BR Clear=right> stops flowing text until there are no more images aligned to the right margin. The above eaxample shows this.

2. <BR Clear=left> stops flowing text until there are no more images aligned to the left margin

3. <BR Clear=all> stops flowing text until there are no more images on either margin – shown below.

Kenyan flag

The Kenyan flag displayed here is stored in GIF format. GIF is a very popular file format for graphics on the internet because of the small amount of storage required.

Some additional text has now been added. You would expect this text text to appear below the flag. This usually is not the case - instead the text will fill the space to the right of the picture on the bottom line of the flag.

8.5   Attaching a link to an image

A link can be attached to an image by nesting the <img> tag within a statement that uses <A href = "link">

Example 22

```
<html>
<head>
     <title>buttons</title>
</head>
<body>
     <h2>Using images as buttons</h2>
     <A href = "feedback.html">
     <img src = "form.jpg" alt = "feedback form"></A>
     <A href = "mylinks.html">
     <img src = "links.jpg" alt = "internet  links"></A>
     <A href = "features.html">
     <img src = "list.jpg" alt = "list of features"></A>
     <A href = "mailto:tonyhawken@talktalk.net">
     <img src = "contact.jpg" alt = "contact me"></A>
</body>
</html>
```

Notes:

1. Buttons like this can be created using Microsoft Paint. Use the rectangle tool to create a small rectangle, Add text, then colour fill the rectangle. Before you save it, crop the picture and save it in jpeg format.

2. Nesting an <img> statement within a <A href> statement will associate a link with a given image.

3. When this image is clicked the link will be activated

8.6   Background colours and colours of links

The following example demonstrates the use of background pictures. It also demonstrates how you can control the colour of links.

Example 23

```
<html>
<head><title>Chemistry resources</title></head>

<body background = "SEAFOAM.gif" text = "black"
     Link = "blue"  vlink = "green" alink = "grey" >

<H4>Chemistry resources</H4>
<P>There follows a selection of notes and other resources
   for the Chemistry student

<P>Offline resources
<OL>
     <li><A href="chem\kin.pdf">Reaction kinetics</A>
     <li><A href="chem\notesh2.doc">Atoms and atomic
          theory</A>
     <li><A href="chem\Ocs05.htm">The alcohols</A>
     <li><A href="#additional">additional notes</A>
</OL>

<P><H4>Online resources</H4>

<OL>
     <li><A href="http://www.knockhardy.org.uk/sci.htm">
         Knockhardy A level Chemistry notes site</A>
     <li><A href="www.knockhardy.org.uk/assets/HALOG.PDF">
          Halogens revision sheet [pdf]</A>
     <li><A href="http://www.knockhardy.org.uk/assets/
          ALCPP.PPT"> Powerpoint presentation on alcohols</A>
     <li><A href="mailto:knockhardy@orpheusmail.co.uk">
          Contact knockhardy by email</A>
</OL>
```

```
<A name ="additional">
<P><H4>Additional notes</H4>
Additional notes can go here.
<P>When I have time I could add some notes within this
    html document.
</body>
</html>
```

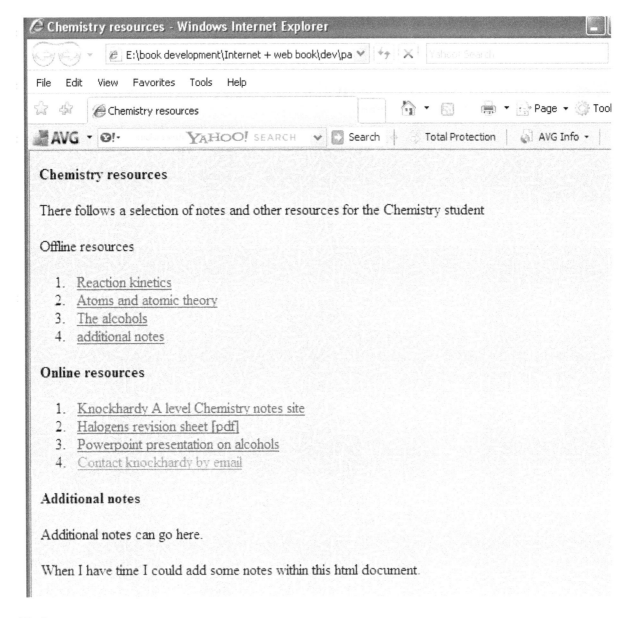

Notes:

1. The <body> tag can take various attributes to specify the properties of various items within the window.

2. The attribute background can be used to specify an image that will act as a background to the window. In this case the image SEAFOAM.gif

3. Instead of having a background image you can specify a background colour. You could for instance use the following within the <body> tag. Bgcolor = "red".

4. Background colours can be mixed. A colour is represented by a 6-digit hexadecimal number. Two digits are required for each colour component – RGB.

5. The **link** attribute refers to links that have never been visited

6. The **vlink** attribute refers to recently visited links

7. The attribute **alink** refers to a link that is at this moment being clicked.

Exercise 8-1

1. The following is an exercise in displaying pictures and text. It also gives you the opportunity to try out various tags and attributes that will affect the layout of text and images.

a Download pictures that show the front covers of a few books. You could have a look at Amazon. Or you could do what I did in question 2, scan books that you own.

b Create a web page that shows a large image of these front covers. Make sure that the image is appropriately sized and takes up a large proportion of the web page. You should also include the ALT tag, so that an appropriate message will be displayed should the image fail to be displayed

c Include appropriate text that describes the book. This should include title, Author, ISBN, date published etc.

d Experiment with the layout of text around the picture. Do you want the text to appear above the picture, or at the bottom of the picture? Also consider whether you want the text to flow around the picture.

e You should also include appropriate headings.

2. Many web sites such as Amazon.co.uk include small images called thumbnails. In this case there are two thumbnails of the front covers of two books that I have written. It is quite common that if you wish to see a larger picture, you click on the thumbnail. Create a web page that recreates the style of what you see below. You can of cause choose to use different books. Make sure that if you click on a thumbnail you load a larger image. (This can easily be achieved by linking the image to another web page that has a larger version of the image).

Books by Tony Hawken

Click on an image to get a larger picture

A course in programming with QBASIC
Tony Hawken
ISBN: 1445240696

A C++ notebook: A first course in programming
Tony Hawken
ISBN: 1445243405

---

3. Modify your web page for question 2. Rather than click on an image to be redirected to a linked page, use traditional links. Write HTML code that will effect the colour of a link depending on whether the link has never been visited, has been visited or has just been clicked on.

8.7 Creating Web page images

There are a number of ways of obtaining images to include in your web pages. These include:

1. Downloading images from the Internet. There are many sites where you are allowed to download images and use them freely.

2. Images can be scanned using a scanner or by using a digital camera.

3. Using a graphical package. You will have to find out what is available or download a free package from the Internet. One to consider is the Open Source software package called GIMP – available from the gnu web site. In the worst-case scenario you will have to use Microsoft Paint.

Image file types

There are three types of graphics file format normally used for storing images on the Internet. These are GIF, JPEG and PNG. A suitable package should be able to store the image in one of these formats. The most important characteristic that is common to these file types is a small file size. This is most important, as graphic images can potentially take up considerable storage – much more than the text for the entire web page. A large file size makes for a very slow download.

Transparency

It is possible to make part of an image transparent - only works for GIF format files. Many graphics packages allow you to do this. This usually involves changing one of the colours used in the image to a clear transparent colour.

Interlace graphics

Graphics files typically are large compared to text files. This makes them slower to download over the Internet. To avoid waiting a long time for an image to appear it is possible to display a rough draft and fill in the detail afterwards. In most cases this means downloading every third line of graphics, and when this is complete download the remaining lines of graphics.

8.8 Graphics file formats

All of the image formats discussed here use bitmap graphics. That is, an image is stored as a huge collection of individual picture elements or pixels that are arranged in rows and columns on the screen. Obviously the higher the resolution, the more pixels you will have on the screen, so more storage will be required. For web graphics a small file size is required, as a large file size dramatically increases the time take to download graphic images.

As an experiment, I took a cropped screen dump that I have included in this book. It was pasted and cropped using Microsoft Paint. It was originally saved as a bitmap. I then opened the picture and saved it in gif and jpeg format.

Above I have included icons for each of the graphic images as they appeared in my folder.

They are as follows:

1. Bitmap (.bmp). This is the original format used by Microsoft Paint. It is characterized by its large file size (1.03 MB)

Both GIF and JPEG format use compression. JPEG compression works by splitting the picture into smaller squares and then by removing pixels where there is only a minor variation in colour. So JPEG compression is lossy (i.e some detail is lost), but if applied carefully this detail isn't very noticeable.

GIF images are best for images where there is a lot of solid colour. So this format is ideal for headings and buttons etc. Whereas JPEG is much better for photos etc.

2. GIF (.gif). The original bitmap can be converted to this format within Microsoft Paint. The file size was much smaller (22.6 KB), but the resolution was much poorer.

3. JPEG (.jpg). The original bitmap file can also be converted to this format. The file size is much smaller (28.1 KB), and with no noticeable degradation of the quality of the picture.

I should note, that the figures given here are also a property of the graphics package used (Microsoft Paint). If you were to use some other package such as Corel Draw, you could expect to get different results.

Clearly the above is an indication that .bmp files should never be found in web pages as they are clearly far too large.

A newer format is now available – PNG. This has the best features of JPEG and GIF.

8.9   Using image maps

An image map enables you to identify a particular region within an image, which can be clicked on with a mouse. Any region so identified can be attached to a hyperlink. The page associated with such a link is thus loaded when the region is clicked on.

Example 24

```
<html>
<head> <title>UK map </title> </head>
<body>
<map name = "ukmap">
<area shape="rect" coords ="350,430,380,450" href
        ="oxford.html">
<area shape="rect" coords ="395,440,420, 460" href
        ="london.html">
<area shape="rect" coords ="435,455,460,475"href
                        ="canterbury.html">
</map>
<img src = "ukmap.gif" usemap = #ukmap>
</body>
</html>
```

An image like the one below can be downloaded from the Internet or scanned in from an atlas. You can then crop the image in a basic graphics package such as Microsoft Paint. The location of where you want to position your hot spots can be determined by using your mouse as a pointer whilst in Paint. You can then estimate the co-ordinates of the rectangle that you wish to identify.

Image of a map showing a hot spot that has been clicked

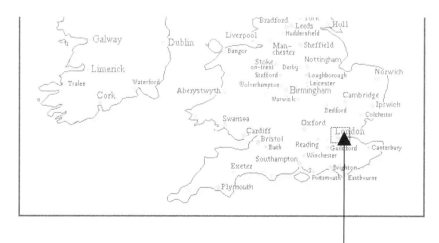

This region has been clicked

135

Notes:

1. The <area> tag is used to identify a given region within an image, and associate with it a hyperlink.

2. In the example above rectangular regions are used. The co-ordinates given refer to the bottom-left and top-right portion of the rectangle.

3. The usemap attribute within the <img> tag associates an image map with an image.

4. Non-rectangular regions an also be used. The following are examples:

```
<Area shape = "circle" coords = "100, 150, 30" href
= "circle.html">

<Area shape = "poly" coords = "100, 150, 120, 180, 175,
200" href = "poly.html">
```

5. In the case of a circular region, the first two numbers represents the position of the centre of the circle. The third number is the radius of the circle.

Exercise 8-2

1. Graphics file formats

(a) List the main graphics formats that are likely to be found in web pages.

(b) What common characteristic do all graphics files have?

(c) For each graphics format describe their characteristics and state in what situations they are likely to be used.

(d) Search on the web for sites that have a lot of images. What file formats are these images stored in? What type of images are they, and why do you think that the given file format was chosen?

2. Obtain a picture of a group of people. This could be obtained from the Internet, or else you could scan a photo of yourself and friends. Create an image map so that you can tag your friends. In this case you could link to another page that gives details about the person clicked on.

Chapter 9 (week 9)

HTML Assignment

9.1 Assignment specification

Assignment 2

Web Site Development (HTML)

In this assignment you will be required to write about various aspects about the World Wide Web and the use of HTML to create web pages. You will also be required to produce your own personal web pages.

Task 1

1. Create a directory called **Unit 2**. Save into this directory all documents that you either create or download whilst doing this assignment.

2. Write a short history outlining the development of the World-Wide-Web.

3. Write a paragraph that explains the importance of the World-Wide-Web.

Task 2

1. Enter the URL: http://infolab.stanford.edu/~ullman/ into the address bar. Click on the link "Books" and obtain a screen dump showing a list of the books he writes.

2. View the source code of this page and obtain a listing of the source code. Edit this listing so that there are no more than 50 lines. Alternatively you could obtain a screen dump showing about 30 lines of text and code.

3. Identify at least 6 different tags within this listing. Describe what they do.

Task 3

1. Download a small picture of your national flag.

2. From the site http://www.grsites.com/textures/ download one or more textures that you would like to use as background images.

3. Describe the main graphics formats used by web sites on the Internet.

Task 4

1. Create an HTML file called **pictures.html**. Edit this file with notepad and insert two pictures – A picture of yourself and the flag you downloaded. Make sure that the pictures are properly sized and that you use the ALT attribute appropriately.

2. Add appropriate text to describe these pictures. You should also experiment with alignment of text around the pictures - center, left and right.

3. Locate a web-site that includes information about your favourite music group. Add a link to this site.

4. Obtain a screen dump of pictures.html and also a printout of the source-code.

Task 5

You will be required to create a personal homepage.

1. Create a new HTML document - call it **homepage.html**. Edit this using notepad and include a large heading "Curriculum Vitae"

2. Where possible add the following information in an unordered list:

    Name, address, telephone number, nationality, date-of-birth, National Insurance number.

Note: *If you are worried about divulging personal information you can make up this information.*

3. Include an Anchor point at the top of the document called "Top".

4. Use a horizontal ruler to underline this section of personal information.

5. Add another section that includes details of your education to date. Include information about the units studied this year at your College.

6. Add another horizontal ruler after this section.

7. Write a personal statement underneath the horizontal ruler. This should have a heading and should also be formatted appropriately in paragraphs. You should also experiment using different fonts, size of text and colour.

8. Reproduce the personal statement using Microsoft Word. Save it in a file called **statement.doc**.

9. Create three links at the bottom of the document. The first should link to the top of the page, the second should link to your word document and the third should link to pictures.html.

10.   Add an email link to one of your teachers.

11.   Modify this page so that one of your images is used as a background.

12.   Obtain a screen dump of this html document and also print out the HTML code.

Task 6

1. Create an HTML document called **misc.html**. Edit this and include a large heading – Bits and bobs.

2. Modify the BODY tag so that the background colour is changed.

3. Create an ordered list. In it include at least two special symbols.

4. Create a definition list. In it define the terms Internet, and World Wide Web.

5. Create a nested list, consisting of an ordered list with one or more unordered lists inside it. The content of these lists is entirely up to you.

6. Produce the following equation in HTML: $\log_{10}a^2 = 2\log_{10}a$.

7. Obtain a screen dump and listing of the file misc.html.

9.2   Task 1

History of the development of the world wide web

See section 6.1.1 (page 83)

The importance of the world wide web

See section 6.1.2 (page 85)

9.3 Task 2

1. screen dump of web page

Jeff Ullman: Book Information

Contents

- Introduction to Automata and Language Theory
- Database Systems: The Complete Book
- A First Course in Database Systems
- Database System Implementation
- Elements of ML Programming
- Foundations of CS/Pascal Edition
- Foundations of CS/C Edition
- Principles of Database and Knowledge-Base Systems
- Compilers: Principles, Techniques, and Tools (aka "The Dragon Book")
- Future Book on Data Mining

2. screen dump of source code

```
Source of: http://infolab.stanford.edu/%7Eullman/ullman-books.html - Mozilla Firefox

File  Edit  View  Help

<HEAD>
<TITLE>Jeffrey D. Ullman --- Books</TITLE>
</HEAD>

<BODY BGCOLOR="E0F7F0">

<H1 ALIGN=CENTER>Jeff Ullman: Book Information</H1>

<H2>Contents</H2>

<UL>
<LI><A HREF = "#hmu">Introduction to Automata and Language Theory</A>
<LI><A HREF = "#dscb">Database Systems: The Complete Book</A>
<LI><A HREF = "#fcdb">A First Course in Database Systems</A>
<LI><A HREF = "#dbsi">Database System Implementation</A>
<LI><A HREF = "#emlp">Elements of ML Programming</A>
<LI><A HREF = "#fcsp">Foundations of CS/Pascal Edition</A>
<LI><A HREF = "#fcsc">Foundations of CS/C Edition</A>
<LI><A HREF = "#pdks">Principles of Database and Knowledge-Base Systems</A>
<LI><A HREF = "#dragon">Compilers: Principles, Techniques, and
Tools (aka "The Dragon Book")</A>
<LI><A HREF = "#mining">Future Book on Data Mining</A>
</UL>
<P>
<A NAME = "grad"></A>
<HR>
<P>
<H2>Gradiance Automated Homeworks</H2>

<A HREF = "http://www.gradiance.com">Gradiance
Corporation</A>
provides their automated homework
system for several of these books, and some others as well.
This service lets students work conventional problems in
subjects such as compilers, and tests their knowledge by random
sampling of their work --- via multiple choice.
Moreover, we turn homework
into a learning experience, since using our "root-question" technology,
students who answer a question wrongly can be given a hint and allowed
to try exactly the same question again.
```

3. List tags within listing

You should be familiar with the following tags:

<HEAD>, <TITLE>, <BODY>, <H1>. <H2>, <UL>, <LI>, <P>, <A>

I have left this as an exercise. All you need to do is write a sentence or two about each tag. All of the information you require is in this book. There are also two different uses of the tag <A>. You could describe them.

Had you included a longer listing, you may well have found other tags with which you are familiar.

9.4 Task 3

1 + 2. Download pictures and textures

3.   Describe main graphics formats. See section 8.8 and research on the Internet.

9.5 Task 4

Example 25

```
<html>
<head><title>Pictures</title></head>
<body>

<H1> Pictures </H1>
<P align = center>
<B>Charles Dangerfield</B>
</P>
<img src = "Cdangerfield2.jpg" height = 300 width = 250
  align = right Alt= "Picture of Charles Dangerfield">
<P>
<Font size = 6>
    This is a picture of myself - head and shoulders.
    In this picture you can see that my hair wants to
    stick up. I think I am overdue a haircut. This picture
    was taken in 2010. It was taken in our front sitting
    room, against a background of yellow.
<P>

<P align = center>
<B>Union Jack</B>
</P>
    <img src = "UnionJack.gif" height = 200 width = 300
    align = left alt = "Union Jack">
    I was born in Croydon, so that makes me English. I could
    have found the English flag, but instead located the
    Union Jack. So I guess I am British - that is a fact.
<P>
    My favourite band is black eyed peas. The link below is
    to the official Black eyed peas web site.
    <A href = "http://www.blackeyedpeas.com/">Music Link</A>

</body>
</html>
```


Notes:

1. A title has been included. You see this title in the tab above the web page.

142

2. Aligning text around an image is really difficult. How the text appears depends on the size of the web pages. If the web page is too narrow, the appearance can be awful.

3. The ALT attribute has been used for both images. In the case of the top picture, the mouse was hovering over the picture. This results in the ALT message being displayed.

4. The link to the favourite band appears as "Music Link".

Screen dump of pictures.html

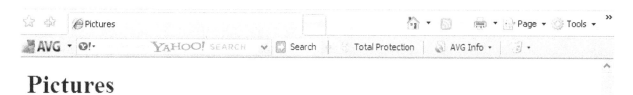

Pictures

Charles Dangerfield

This is a picture of myself - head and shoulders. In this picture you can see that my hair wants to stick up. I think I am overdue a haircut. This picture was taken in 2010. It was taken in our front sitting room, against a background of yellow.

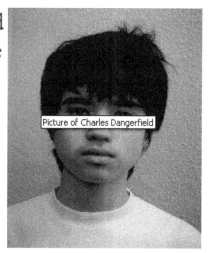

Picture of Charles Dangerfield

Union Jack

I was born in Croydon, so that makes me English. I could have found the English flag, but instead located the Union Jack. So I guess I am British - that is a fact.

My favourite band is black eyed peas. The link below is to the official Black eyed peas web site. Music Link

9.6 Task 5

<u>Example 26</u>

```
<html>
<head><title>homepage unit 2</title> </head>
<body background = "yello014.jpg">
<A name = "Top">
<H1>Curriculum Vitae</H1>
<UL>
      <LI> Name: Charles Dangerfield
      <LI> Address : 42 London road, Croydon
      <LI> telephone: 0208 686 4356
      <LI> dob: 23/06/1990
      <LI> nationality: British
      <LI> NI#: WA1080B
</UL>
<HR size = 5 width = 70% color = blue>
<H1>Education to date</H1>
Education entered in reverse chrononological order
<P>
<B>Croydon college (sep 2008 - Jul 2009) </B>
<P>
BTEC National - ICT Practitioners
<BR> Disticions for most modules
<P>
<B>Harris CTC (Sep 2002 - Jun 2008)</B>
<p>
8 GCSEs including English and Mathematics
(3Cs, 4Ds and 1Es)
<P>
<HR size = 5 width = 70% color = blue>
<H1> Personal statement </H1>
<P>
<FONT FACE = "aeriel" size = 4 color = "blue">
I am a keen student with nearly 100% attendance. I excel at
ICT. I have completed a BTEC first for IT practitioners,
gaining mostly distinctions in the modules. The modules that I
enjoyed most were those that involved web design. The web
design on the Access programme is much more practical, and in
many ways more relevant.
</FONT>
<P><H1> Useful links </H1>
Go to top of page <A href = "#Top">Top of page</A>
<P>
Personal statement (WORD version) <A href = "statement.doc">
Personal statement</A>
<P>
Email my teacher <A href = "mailto:tony_hawken@talktalk.net">
Email teacher</A>

</body>
</html>
```

Notes:

1. The text in this example was deliberately kept short, so that the resulting web page is small. Small enough to obtain a screen dump and crop it in PAINT.

2. The Curriculum Vitae is also fictitious. Even if students use their real name, they probably don't want other people to know about their exam results.

3. The tag <FONT> was used to change the characteristics of the text. Alternatively you could add attributes to the <P> tag to affect changes in the text.

screen dump of homepage

Curriculum Vitae

- Name: Charles Dangerfield
- Address : 42 London road, Croydon
- telephone: 0208 686 4356
- dob: 23/06/1990
- nationality: British
- NI#: WA1080B

Education to date

Education entered in reverse chrononological order

Croydon college (sep 2008 - Jul 2009)

BTEC National - ICT Practitioners
Disticions for most modules

Harris CTC (Sep 2002 - Jun 2008)

8 GCSEs including English and Mathematics (3Cs, 4Ds and 1Es)

Personal statement

I am a keen student with nearly 100% attendance. I excel at ICT. I have completed a BTEC first for IT practitioners, gaining mostly distinctions in the modules. The modules that I enjoyed most were those that involved web design. The web design on the Access programme is much more practical, and in many ways more relevant.

Useful links

Go to top of page Top of page

Personal statement (WORD version) Personal statement

Email my teacher Email teacher

Done   My Computer   100%

9.7 Task 6

Source code of misc.html

<u>Example 27</u>

```
<html>
<head><title>Odds and Sods</title></head>
<body bgcolor = yellow>

<h1>Bits and bobs</H1>

<OL>
    <LI>My teacher is a &frac12; wit
    <LI>This web page is &copy; Charles Dangerfield 2010
    <LI>4 &#215; 3 + 8 &#247; 2 = 16
</OL>


<DL>
    <DT>Internet
    <DD>World wide collection of linked computer networks
    <DT>World Wide Web
    <DD>World Wide collection of web pages that are stored on
the Internet
</DL>


The main soups that I make at home are:
<OL>
    <LI>Leak and Potato soup - main ingredients are:
    <UL>
        <LI>Leaks (3)
        <LI>Potato (1)
        <LI>Onion (1)
        <LI>Carrot (1)
        <LI>1 pint vegetable stock
        <LI>Salt and pepper
    </UL>
    <LI>Tomato soup - main ingredients are:
    <UL>
        <LI>1 pound of Tomatoes
        <LI>1 potato
        <LI>1 onion
        <LI>&frac34; pint of vegetable stock
        <LI>&frac34; pint of milk
    </UL>
</OL>

log<sub>10</sub>a<sup>2</sup> = 2log<sub>10</sub>a

</body>
</html>
```

Screen dump of misc.html

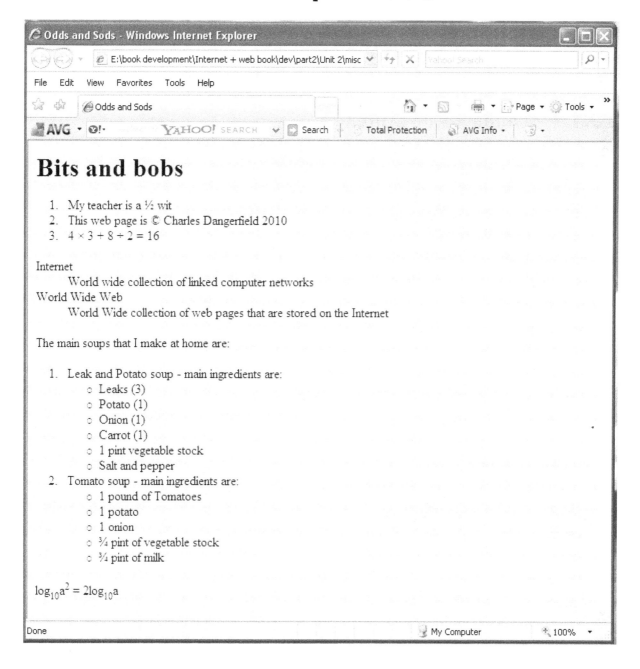

Bits and bobs

1. My teacher is a ½ wit
2. This web page is © Charles Dangerfield 2010
3. $4 \times 3 + 8 \div 2 = 16$

Internet
> World wide collection of linked computer networks

World Wide Web
> World Wide collection of web pages that are stored on the Internet

The main soups that I make at home are:

1. Leak and Potato soup - main ingredients are:
   - Leaks (3)
   - Potato (1)
   - Onion (1)
   - Carrot (1)
   - 1 pint vegetable stock
   - Salt and pepper
2. Tomato soup - main ingredients are:
   - 1 pound of Tomatoes
   - 1 potato
   - 1 onion
   - ¾ pint of vegetable stock
   - ¾ pint of milk

$\log_{10}a^2 = 2\log_{10}a$

Chapter 10 (week 10)

Summary

10.1 Tasks to complete

1. You will have to do some research for this unit, on the World Wide Web. You will be required to write a short History on the World Wide Web. You will also need to appreciate the importance of the Wide World Web and be able to write about this. See section 6.1. Also there is a lot of materials on the Internet. It would be a good idea to create a folder to save relevant materials in. Then anytime you come across something useful you can save the documents found on the Internet to this folder. Also see the bibliography for suggested reading.

2. You will have to do the same thing for graphics file formats, as you will have to be able to write about them as well. See section 8.8.

3. Make sure that you are prepared for creating your own web pages. I suggest that you create a separate folder for this. Also create a shortcut to notepad, so that each time you want to create a new HTML file you can click on this. Remember that it is an HTML file that you want to create, not a text file.

4. If you need any pictures for your web pages, save these in the same folder as the HTML files. Alternatively you could create a folder especially for images.

5. Much of the evidence required to demonstrate that you have carried out the assignment tasks as required, is achieved by creating a screen dump, and cropping it within Paint so that only the relevant bits are kept. This cropped image can then be inserted into a word-processed document. This needs to be done to show that you can obtain source code of a downloaded web site. It also needs to be done to illustrate the appearance of your own web pages.

6. This unit tests your ability at creating a simple web site. You will need to be able to demonstrate that you can create headings, format paragraphs and affect the appearance of text. You will also need to be able to create lists, links to other documents, and be able to insert pictures into a web page. All of this is done by entering text interspersed with HTML commands into a text file that you save with a .html extension.

10.2   Unit Summary

1. The World Wide Web is an enormous collection of linked web pages that are stored on the Internet.

2. The idea of the Internet was invented by Tim Berners-Lee in 1990 whilst working at CERN in Switzerland.

3. Besides conceiving the idea of the Internet, Tim Berners-Lee created the HTTP protocol that specifies how data from the World Wide Web is to be transferred. In fact he created a complete working model that included a web server and web browser.

4. A web browser is an essential tool for accessing the World Wide Web. It can interpret HTML tags and format web pages accordingly.

5. The two most popular browsers are Microsoft Internet Explorer and Mozilla Firefox.

6. Both of these browsers allow you to view the source code of a web page. Microsoft Internet Explorer also incorporates an editor (notepad), so that you can edit web pages as well.

7. To create your own web pages you have 3 types of software tool that you could use. A text editor such as notepad, an HTML editor that helps you with the HTML coding or a WYSIWIG web development package such as Microsoft FrontPage or Adobe Dreamweaver.

8. All HTML files must have the extension .htm or .html.

9. If you create an HTML file with no HTML tags all blank lines and multiple spaces will be removed by your browser.

10.   HTML is a markup language that identifies certain parts of a document such as a paragraph and allows a browser to render it accordingly.

11.   Each HTML document starts with the tag <HTML> and ends with </HTML>. This tells the browser that everything in between is HTML and text.

12.   An HTML document can be thought of consisting of two components – a head and a body. The head is contained between the tags <HEAD> and </HEAD>. The body is contained between the tags <BODY> and </BODY>.

13.   Within the head of a document we can place such things as a title for a web page.

14. Within the body of a web page you place the content of the web page. This is all the text and pictures etc that you wish to display on the screen.

15. A new paragraph is started using the <P> tag. Associated with a paragraph there are a number of attributes. You can specify the font-type, font-size, colour etc. You can also specify a text-indent for the beginning of a paragraph.

16. To start a new line you use the <BR> tag. Unlike a new paragraph there are no blank lines created.

17. There are 6 sizes of headings - <H1>, <H2>, <H3>, <H4>, <H5>, <H6>. The largest size of heading is given with <H1> and the smallest with <H6>. So for a size 1 heading, the text between <H1> and </H1> is used to create a heading on the page.

18. There are a number of ways that you can emphasize text. The most obvious way is to use the tags <B>, <I>, and <U> for bold, italic. and underline.

19. You can also create subscripts and superscripts - <SUB> and <SUP>.

20. An unordered list is the type where each item in the list starts with a bullet point. To start an unordered list you use the tag <UL>. Then for each item in the list you include the tag <LI>.

21. An ordered list is the type that has a number or a letter in from of each list item. You start an ordered list by using the tag <OL>. By default your ordered list will be numbered and start with the number 1.

22. To change the sequence type of a list you use the Type attribute. The value 1 is for ordinary numbers ... 1, 2, 3, 4 etc. The value I is used to denote capital roman numerals I, II, II, IV etc, and the value i is used to denote lower-case Roman numerals i. ii, ii, iv. Alphabetic numbering is used if you use A or a. A is for uppercase and a is for lowercase.

23. A definition list is typically used to produce a glossary. It starts with the tag <DL>. Each item in a definition list is made up of two parts. The term to be defined starts with the tag <DT>. The definition of the term starts with the tag <DD>.

24. You can create hyperlinks to link to other documents either online or on your own computer. A link uses the tag <A>. You need to use the attribute href to identify the location of the document – the URL.

25. You can even link to positions within a given document. To do this you need to create an anchor point within a document. This is done using the <A> tag together with the attribute NAME.

26. You can have links to just about any type of file. You can also link to an email address using mailto.

27. You can insert a picture into a web page using the <IMG> tag. Here the attribute src is used to identify the location of the image file.

28. All images need to be appropriately sized with the height and width attributes. You should also use alt to give information about the picture you intend to display.

29. Text can be made to wrap around a picture. You can use the align attribute to specify where text will appear in relation to the picture.

30. A link can be attached to an image by nesting the <img> tag within a statement that uses <A href = "link">. Clicking on the image will then take you to the linked document.

31. There are 3 main graphics file formats used on the Internet – GIF, JPEG and PNG. All of these formats have one thing in common – they enable you to have pictures with small file sizes.

32. If you insert a picture in your web page, you can create hotspots that link to another document. This is often referred to as an image map.

33. You can specify a background image by using the attribute background within the tag <BODY>. In a similar way you can specify a background colour. This time you use the attribute bgcolor.

34. The attributes link, alink, and vlink can be used to specify the colour of a link a different times. The value link is for a link that has never been visited. The value alink is for a link that has been previously visited, and vlink is for a link that has just been clicked.

Part 3

Further web site development

Aims

After completing this 5-week unit, you will be able to do the following:

Design

Be able to create a site map illustrating how the web pages of a site are to be linked.

Create a storyboard indicating the layout of pages

Style sheets

Understand the importance of style sheets and be able to explain why they would be used on a corporate web site.

Create an external style sheet containing styles for paragraphs, headings, links and background colour.

Be able to create inline style sheets and understand how these can override the styles included in linked style sheets.

Tables

Create simple tables to arrange text in columns (tabular format). Include headings.

Change background colour for individual table cells and be able to insert pictures.

Be able to add table borders and apply cell padding to space data within a table cell.

Forms

Create forms that include a variety of controls to collect data from a user. These should include text boxes, text area, check boxes, radio buttons and pop-down menus.

Be able to specify a form-handler to process the data collected by the form (Your default email program). Use Submit buttons to send the data, or reset button to clear the form.

Chapter 11 (week 11)

Web design and Style sheets

11.1   Elements of design

Web sites normally have a hierarchical structure as indicated on the right. In addition to this, the subsidiary and topic pages will often link back to the homepage and other pages as well.

In a hierarchical organization, visitors can easily know their position in the structure. If they go back they usually go to the previous level.

It is often useful to add additional links, to enable the visitor to go back to previous pages

```
        ┌──────────────┐
        │ Main page    │
        │ (homepage)   │
        └──────────────┘
    ┌──────────┼──────────┐
┌────────┐ ┌────────┐ ┌────────┐
│ Topic 1│ │ Topic 2│ │ Topic 3│
│ #1     │ │ #2     │ │ #3     │
└────────┘ └────────┘ └────────┘
        ┌──────┴──────┐
   ┌──────────┐ ┌──────────┐
   │Subsidiary│ │Subsidiary│
   │page      │ │page      │
   │#2a       │ │  #2b     │
   └──────────┘ └──────────┘
```

Linear organisation

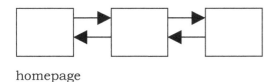

homepage

Hierarchical and linear combination

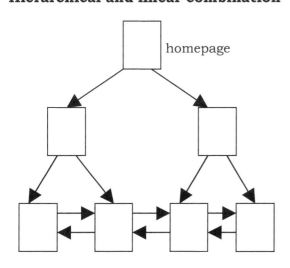

Another way to organize your documents is to use a linear or sequential organization.

This in best used, if the content of the web site would normally be read sequentially like the pages of a book.

Probably the most popular format involves a mixture of both. Note that there are links to go both forward and backwards in the linear part of this design. There probably also ought to be additional links to go back up the hierarchy.

All of these designs can be done in a word-processing package such as Microsoft Word Or OpenOffice and annotated in pencil as required.

Alternatively they can be drawn.

11.2   Design process and storyboards

The design of a web site depends on many factors. For instance you need to consider the target audience, their age range, their computer experience, the subject matter and the impression you want to give users.

Once these questions have been considered, you need to design a layout for the pages you need for the site and determine how they are to link together. **A site map** and a collection of page layouts is referred to as a **storyboard** or **wireframe**. At its simplest, this is just a collection of hand-drawn sketches indicating where various components such as logos, headings, blocks of text, links etc will appear on a page, together with a site map that indicates how the pages are to be linked together. A site map will look like the diagrams on the previous page. Each page in the diagram must have the name of the file corresponding to each web page and arrows indicating how they link to other pages.

Sketch of a homepage

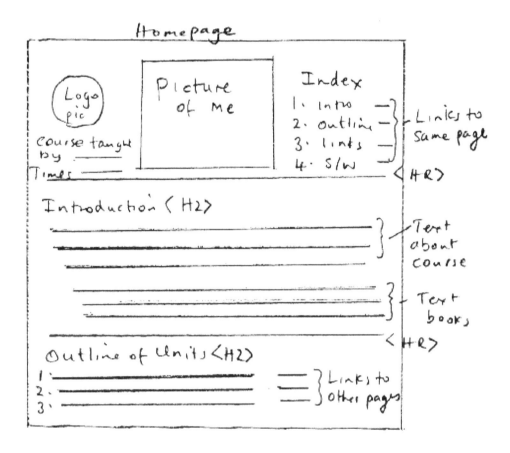

In the same manner, you would be expected to sketch the structure of other pages that will be linked to this homepage. They can be as detailed as you like, or could just give an overall impression of the structure as illustrated above.

This storyboard needs to make it clear how a user is likely to use the site and navigate to other pages by clicking on the links. To achieve this it is important to include a site plan that indicates how the web pages are linked together. This often takes the form of a structure chart as illustrated below.

Site plan for AS mathematics course

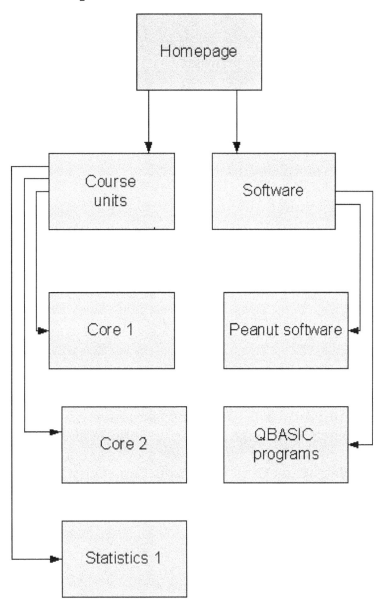

11.3　Documenting your web pages

11.3.1　Use of comments

Comments can be included in HTML source code, and are used in much the same way as in C++ programs. They are there to explain some parts of the HTML code and are not displayed by the browser.

A comment appears between the tags:

```
<!--   and    -->
```

Here is an example of a simple comment.

```
<!-- This is a comment -->
```

And here is another example. This time the comment spans several lines.

```
<!--   This is a multiple
       line comment.
       It ends with the sequence of characters   -->
```

11.3.2　Storyboards

A storyboard, consisting of a site map and sketches or diagrams that represent the page layout for each web page are an essential part of the documentation. These should be printed out, and not just kept on the computer. You may want to adopt a uniform style for each of your web pages. If this is the case you can identify those style features that are common to your web pages. This common style can then be provided by means of an external style sheet that can be loaded by each page.

11.3.3　Document type definitions

To comply with the standards of the W3C, the following should always be the first line of all HTML documents if you are using Strict HTML 4.01.

```
<!DOCTYPE HTML PUBLIC "-//W3C//DTD HTML 4.01//EN"
  "http://www.w3.org/TR/html4/strict.dtd">
```

This is a particular requirement if you intend to use the W3C validation service.

Exercise 11-1

In this exercise you will design the layout of a personal web site that contains at least 5 linked web pages. It should include a homepage that has general information about yourself. This web page should also link to other pages and documents. The other web pages could include one for education, another for interests and hobbies, a personal statement etc.

1. Create an outline sketch of how you want the homepage to appear. You should include headings, paragraphs of text, images and links etc.

2. Think about the style that you want to adopt for headings and paragraphs. At this stage you will have to decide on font-type, font size, indentation, and colour etc. Write this information down, as it can be used to create an external style sheet.

3. Create an outline sketch for at least one of the other web pages. If you want to change the style of a number of web elements you will need to be able to identify how these are different from the style to be adopted for the homepage. This information can then be used for putting together an embedded style sheet to override the style specified by the external style sheet.

4. Create a structure chart to indicate the relationship between web pages. That is how are the pages to be linked, and how do you expect a user to navigate your web site. You could use the Drawing tool within OpenOffice to do this.

11.4   An introduction to style sheets

11.4.1   What is a style sheet?

HTML was originally intended as a mark-up language to provide content rather than appearance. Various vendors such as Netscape provided non-standard attributes to many of the tags to affect the appearance of the web page.

Most of these attributes are now standard in HTML 4. The problem is that the addition of all these attributes makes coding much more cumbersome and slows downloading.

The introduction of cascading style sheets provides a means of separating the content of the web site from the layout. All detailed about layout - how to present paragraphs etc, is now put into a style sheet. HTML documents then link to a particular style sheet

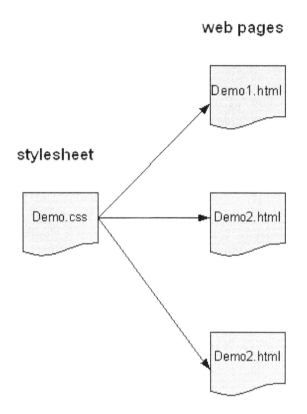

Each tag within HTML has a number of properties or attributes associated with it. Within a style sheet, you specify a **style** for the main tags that you intend to use. A **style** is merely a set of rules that tell a browser how to display a particular HTML tag. So, the rules applied within a style sheet replace the attributes associated with tags in HTML. This makes HTML coding much easier.

11.4.2   Types of Style sheets

There are three types of style sheet:

1. **Inline style sheet.** The inline method allows you to take existing HTML tags and add a style to it. This is achieved by using the **style** attribute within the tag. The most commonly used tag for this purpose is the paragraph tag <P>. A style attribute within a paragraph tag can be used to control the characteristics of the text within that paragraph.

2. **Embedded style sheet.** The embedded method allows you to control the entire HTML page. This requires the use of the **<style>** tag which is placed between the **<html>** and **<body>** tags. Using <style> tags it is possible to control the text style for the whole document. To separate the style sheet from the body of the HTML code and text, it is common to place the style sheet in the header of the HTML document.

3. **Linked or external style sheet.** A linked style sheet is an external document that specifies specific text format styles. This external document can be referenced by many HTML documents. In this manner it is possible to have a consistent style for all the HTML documents on your web-site.

   To create an external style sheet, you open a text document within an editor such as notepad and save the file with a filename that has the file extension .css. As with HTML files you need to make sure that you click on the all files option to make sure that it is not saved as a text document with a .txt file extension. If you have created a style sheet successfully, it should look like this.

The above icon, is the one created in section 11.7.

159

11.5   Inline style

The following example demonstrates the use of the **style** attribute within a paragraph tag. The **span** tag can be used to change the style of part of a document – in this case the end of the paragraph.

Example 28

```
<html>
<head>
<title>inline style sheets 1</title>
</head>
<body>
<H1>THE MOUNTAIN IN LABOUR</H1>                    <BR>FABLE 10
<p style = "font: 18pt Bookman">
    In the days of yore, a mighty rumbling was heard in a
    Mountain. It was said to be in labour, and multitudes flocked
    Together from far and near, to see what it would produce.
<span style = "font: 12pt Wide Latin">
    After long expectation and many wise conjectures from the
    bystanders - out popped a Mouse!    </P>
<P>
    The story applies to those whose magnificent promises end in
    a paltry performance.
</body>
</html>
```

THE MOUNTAIN IN LABOUR

FABLE 10

In the days of yore, a mighty rumbling was heard in a Mountain. It was said to be in labour, and multitudes flocked Together from far and near, to see what it would produce. After long expectation and many wise conjectures from the bystanders - out popped a Mouse!

The story applies to those whose magnificent promises end in a paltry performance.

Notes:

1. In the first new paragraph the font type is changed from the default font to 18pt Bookman.

2. The <Span style> tag is used to change characteristics within a paragraph. In the above example the font type is changed to 12pt Wide Latin.

3. In the next new paragraph the font style reverts back to the default.

11.6   Embedded Style sheets

Embedded style sheets use the <style> tag.

<u>Example 29</u>

```
<html>
<head>
<title>inline style sheets 1</title>

<style>
BODY      {background: #FFFFFF; color: #000000; margin-top:
            0.25in; margin-left: 0.75in; margin-right: 0.75in}
H1    {font: 14pt Verdanna; color: #0000FF}
P     {font: 12pt Bookman; text-indent: 0.5in}
</style>

</head>

<body>
<H1>THE MOUNTAIN IN LABOUR</H1>                    <BR>FABLE 10
<P>
      In the days of yore, a mighty rumbling was heard in a
      Mountain. It was said to be in labour, and multitudes flocked
      together from far and near, to see what it would produce.
      After long expectation and many wise conjectures from the
      bystanders - out popped a Mouse!    </P>
<P>
      The story applies to those whose magnificent promises end in
      a paltry
performance.
</body>
</html>
```

Notes:

1. Within the style tags you define the properties of other tags. For example <body>, <P>, and <H1>.

2. A group of properties for each tag are contained within curly braces.

3. The tag BODY is used to specify the layout of the entire web page. The background colour is set to white, the colour of the text is set to black, and the top, left and right margins are set using inches.

4. The HI heading has the font set to blue 14 point Verdanna. This is rather small for a H1 heading.

5. The text within each paragraph can also be determined by the style sheet. In this case the font is set to 12 point Bookman. This text will be black as this

colour has been set by the tag BODY, and it has not been overridden. Also each time a new paragraph starts it is indented 0.5 inches.

How the web page appears

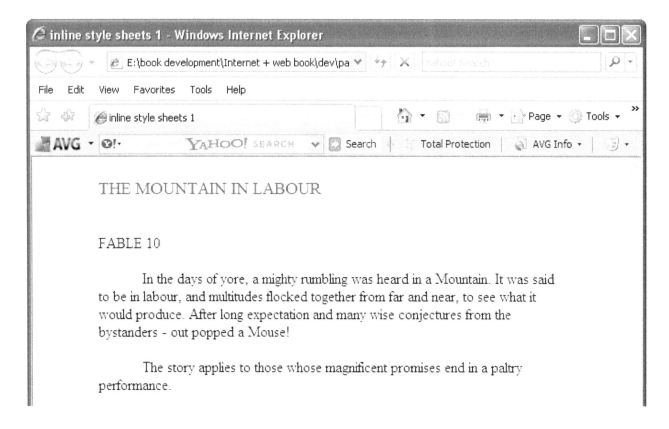

11.7   Use of external style sheets

The following is an example of a cascading style sheet. This was saved as **mystyle.css** and can be accessed by an HTML document. This style sheet is concerned with 3 aspects of the html document: BODY, H1 headings and paragraphs.

Example 30

```
<!--
BODY        {background: #FFFFFF; color: #000000; margin-top:
             0.25in; margin-left: 0.75in; margin-right: 0.75in}
H1          {font: 14pt Verdanna; color: #0000FF}
P           {font: 12pt Bookman; text-indent: 0.5in}
-->
```

The following HTML document links to the above style sheet. Collectively these two files do the same job as the previous example. Below the link tag is used to link to a style sheet.

Example 31

```
<html>
<head>
<title>inline style sheets 1</title>
<link rel = stylesheet href = "mystyle.css" type = "text/css">
</head>
<body>
<H1>THE MOUNTAIN IN LABOUR</H1>                      <BR>FABLE 10
<P>
    In the days of yore, a mighty rumbling was heard in a
    Mountain. It was said to be in labour, and multitudes flocked
    together from far and near, to see what it would produce.
    After long expectation and many wise conjectures from the
    bystanders - out popped a Mouse!
<P>
The story applies to those whose magnificent promises end in a
paltry performance.
</body>
</html>
```

Notes:

1. The style sheet above is equivalent to the embedded style sheet in section 11.6. The only difference is that it is stored in a different file.

2. The advantage of having external style sheets is that more than one html file can link to them. This is a useful feature if you want to adopt a uniform style for all pages in a given web site. It also makes for less work.

11.8   Style attributes for paragraphs

The following are examples of commonly used style attributes for paragraphs:

font: This attribute lets you set many properties at the same time

These properties can be set separately using the following:

font-family   This is used to name the font you want to use.

font-size: You can use this to specify the font-size in inches, cm or points.

```
e.g.   {font-size: 12pt}

       {font-size: 0.75in}

       {font-size: 2cm}
```

font-weight: This is used to determine the thickness of a character
                        Instead of using the font-weight attribute the following can be
                        used instead:

extra-light, demi-light, light, medium, extra-bold, demi-bold, bold

text-decoration: This attribute decorates text with options such as :-

```
none, underline, italic, line-through
```

line-height: This sets the amount of space between lines of text. The size
                 can be specified using points, inches or cm.

```
e.g.   P {line-height: 14pt}
```

margin-left: used to set left margin. (points, inches or centimetres).

margin-right: used to set right margin. (points, inches or centimetres).

margin-top: used to set top margin. (points, inches or centimetres).

text-indent: indent the text. (points, inches or centimetres).

text-align: This allows you to justify the text. (left, right or center)

background: used to set background colour or use background graphics

Below is an example of how some of the above attributes can be used.

```
P { font-family: Courier; font-size: 12pt; font-weight: demi-bold;
    text-align: center; background: mybackground.gif}
```

11.9 Another linked style sheet example

Example 32

```
<!--
BODY
{
    Background-color : black;

    H1, H2, H3, H4, H5, H6  { font-family : "Times New Roman";
                              font-style : italic;
                              color : blue                    }



    P { text-indent : 2cm;
        text-align : justify;
        color: white;
        font-family : Aerial, Helvetica;
        font-size : medium;                    }

    A:link { color : blue }
    A:active  { color : red }
    A:visited  {color : green }

    BLOCKQUOTE {width 60%;
            border: solid white;
            color : green                    }

}
-->
```

Notes:

1. The font-family, font-style and color is determined for any type of heading.

2. Text-indent, text-align, color, font-family and font-size are determined for all paragraphs.

3. Text-align can have possible values – left, right, center, and justify.

4. Font-size can have the following values – xx-small, x-small, small, medium, large, x-large, xx-large, or alternatively can be given a measurement.

5. A font can be assigned a font-weight. This can have values – Normal, bold, bolder, lighter, 100, 200, 300, 400, 500, 600, 700, 800, 900.

6. Font-family can take the values – Times New Roman, Aerial, serif, sans-serif, monospace.

7.   Font-style can take the values - Normal, italic, oblique.

8.   The characteristics of links are determined by stating the attributes of A:link, A:active, A:visited. As well as changing the colour you can also determine other font characteristics.

9.   Whatever occurs within a blockquote is normally indented. This can be boxed in, by specifying a border. The border itself, and the text within it, can be given certain characteristics.

This is how the web page in section 11.10 appears using the previous style sheet and rendered with Internet Explorer.

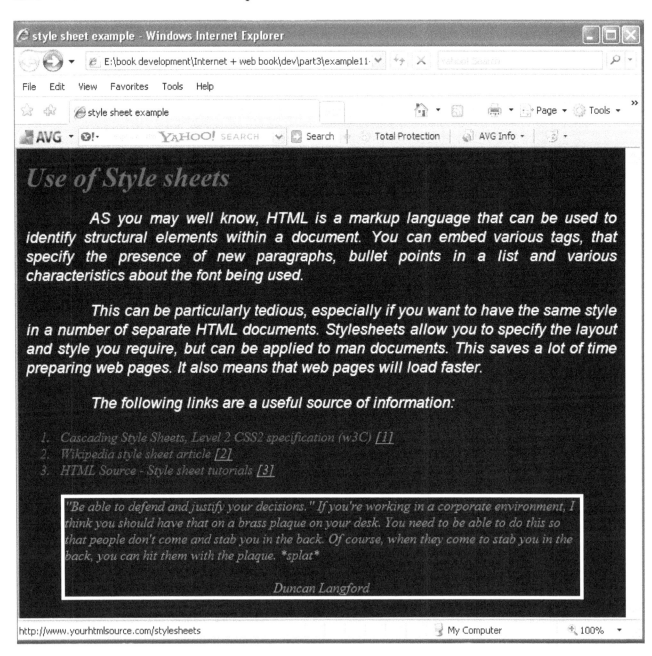

11.10 Corresponding HTML file with minimal formatting

Example 33

```
<html>
<head>
<title>style sheet example</title>
<link rel = stylesheet href = "style1.css" type = "text/css">
</head>
<body>
<H1>Use of Style sheets</H1>
<P>
    AS you may well know, HTML is a markup language that can be
    used to identify structural elements within a document. You
    can embed various tags, that specify the presence of new
    paragraphs, bullet points in a list and various
    characteristics about the font being used.
<P>
    This can be particularly tedious, especially if you want to
    have the same style in a number of separate HTML documents.
    Stylesheets allow you to specify the layout and style you
    require, but can be applied to man documents. This saves a
    lot of time preparing web pages. It also means that web pages
    will load faster.
<P>
    The following links are a useful source of information:
<OL>
    <LI> Cascading Style Sheets, Level 2 CSS2 specification (w3C)
        <A href = "http://www.w3.org/TR/REC-CSS2/">[1]</A>
    <LI> Wikipedia style sheet article
        <A href =
            "http://en.wikipedia.org/wiki/Style_Sheet">[2]</A>
    <LI> HTML Source - Style sheet tutorials
       <A href =
            "http://www.yourhtmlsource.com/stylesheets">[3]</A>
</OL>
<P>
<BLOCKQUOTE>
    "Be able to defend and justify your decisions." If you're
    working in a corporate environment, I think you should have
    that on a brass plaque on your desk. You need to be able to
    do this so that people don't come and stab you in the back.
    Of course, when they come to stab you in the back, you can
    hit them with the plaque. *splat*
    <P><center>
    Duncan Langford
</BACKQUOTE>

</body>
</html>
```

167

11.11   The CSS box model

The CSS box model is often represented as a number of concentric rectangular boxes that can be used to represent all HTML elements. Normally the box model is represented by border, padding and content. You can then specify the size of this. Optionally, you can then add a margin around this. Once a box width has been determined, you can specify the thickness of margin, border and padding.

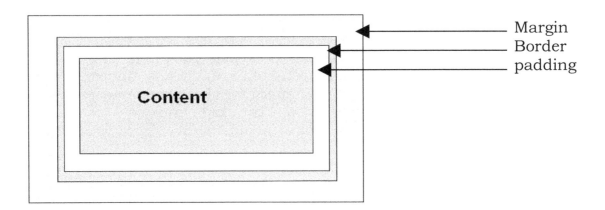

The following examples will all use the same basic HTML file, and will then load different style sheets.

Example 34

```
<HTML>
<HEAD>
     <TITLE>Aesop fable 10</TITLE>

</HEAD>
<BODY>
<H2>THE MOUNTAIN IN LABOUR</H2>
<BR>FABLE 10
<P>
In the days of yore, a mighty rumbling was heard in a Mountain. It
was said to be in labour, and multitudes flocked together from far
and near, to see what it would produce. After long expectation and
many wise conjectures from the bystanders - out popped a Mouse!
<P>
The story applies to those whose magnificent promises end in a
paltry performance.
</BODY>
</HTML>
```

This document has a single heading and two paragraphs. We will then apply a number of style sheets to this document. To apply a style sheet we need to add a line such as:

```
<link rel = stylesheet href = "style1.css" type = "text/css">
```

With no style sheet this web page looks like this:

Screen dump for basic web page (no style sheets)

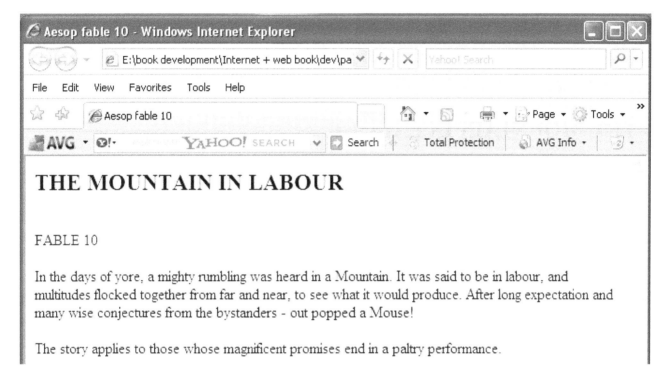

The following examples style sheets will be linked to the same html file.

11.11.1 Margins

<u>Example 35</u>

```
<!--
p    { margin-top: 0.5cm;
       margin-bottom: 0.5cm;
       margin-left: 1cm;
       margin-right: 1cm}

h2   { margin-bottom: 0.75cm }
-->
```

Notes:

1. Margins can be applied to individual sides of the box.

2. In this example the units are in cm. I could have used ems or px, mm, in.

3. 1em is the width of an uppercase M in the current font type and font size.

4. The unit px refers to pixels or picture units.

Screen dump for example 35

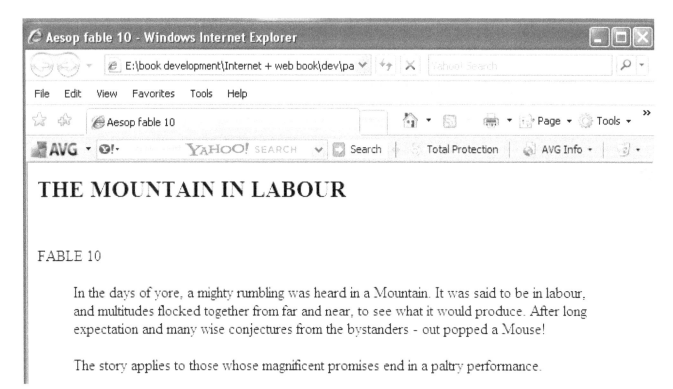

Example 36

```
<!--
p    { margin: 1cm }

h2   { margin-bottom: 0.75cm }
-->
```

Notes:

1. In this example all the margins for a paragraph are set at 1cm. This shorthand avoids the need to specify separately margin-top, margin-left, margin-right and margin-bottom.

2. If two values are set for margin:, the first value is for margin-top and margin-bottom. The second value is use to set the values for margin-left and margin-right.

3. Example code for two values could look like this:

    P   { margin: 1cm 1.5cm }

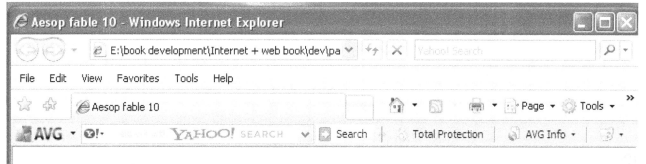

11.11.2 Padding

Example 37

```
<!--
p     { padding: 1cm }

h2    { padding-right: 0.75cm;
        padding-top: 0.5cm     }
-->
```

Notes:

1. In this example padding has been applied to both paragraphs and size 2 headings.

2. For paragraphs, padding of 1 cm is applied to each edge of the box.

3. For size two headings, padding has been applied to the right and top edges of the box.

4. In this example applying padding to the right edge makes no sense.

5. If I wanted different size padding for a paragraph, I could have used the following short-hand code to specify sizes for top, left, right and bottom:

P { padding: 1cm 1.25cm 1.25cm 0.75cm }

Screen dump for example 37

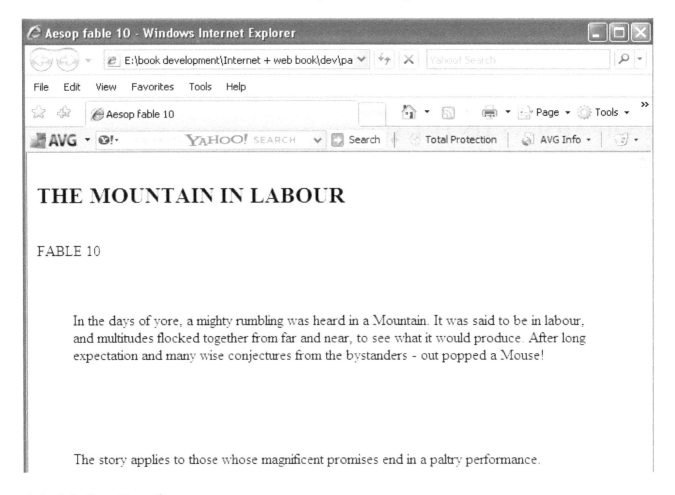

11.11.3   Borders

Example 38

```
<!--
p    { border-top: 1px solid blue;
       border-left: 1px solid blue;
       border-right: 1px solid blue;
       border-bottom: 1px solid blue }

h2   { border: 2px solid green      }
-->
```

Notes:

1. A 1 pixel border blue border is specified for each edge of the box containing a paragraph.

2. The most appropriate unit for a border is px, though you could if you wanted use other units.

3. I could have used a short cut to specify this:

    P   { border: 1px solid blue }

4. H2 headings are given a green border 2 pixels in size.

Screen dump example 38

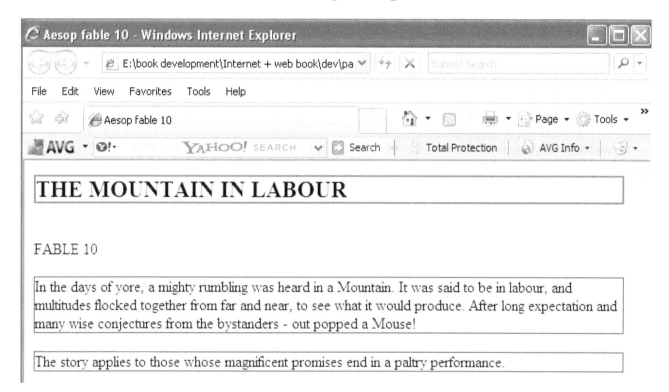

Example 39

```
<!--
p     { border: 1px solid blue;
        width: 60mm; }

h2    { border: 2px solid green      }
-->
```

Notes:

1. In this example the width of a paragraph has been specified. In this case 60mm.

2. I could have specified the height.

3. A border is included to emphasize the size of the content.

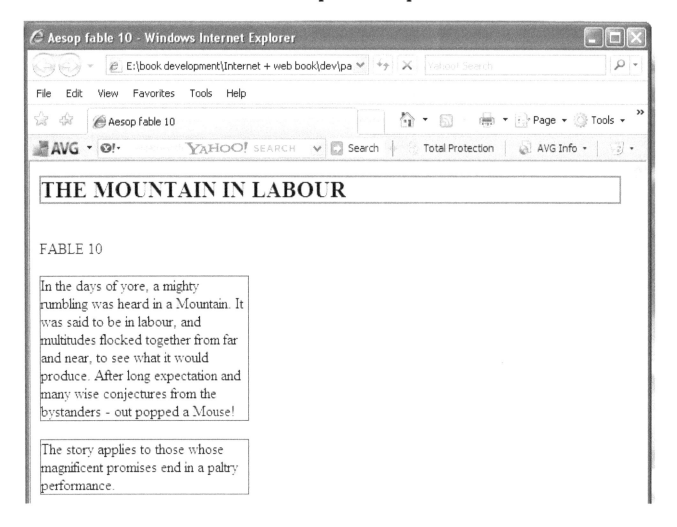

11.11.4 Back-ground colour

Example 40

```
<!--
p       {background-color: yellow }

h2      { background-color: gray }
-->
```

Notes:

1. The background colour can be set to any element you choose. In this case the background colour for paragraphs is yellow, and size 2 headings are grey.

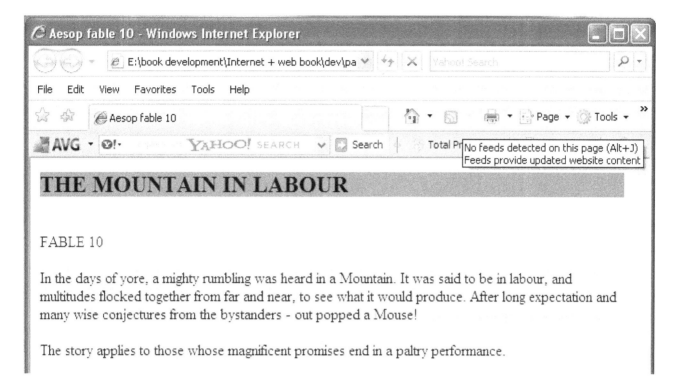

11.12 Advantages of Style sheets

A style sheet enables you to store all the information about presentation in one file. This means that it takes less time to create web pages, as you can provide the minimum of formatting instructions within the HTML document. It also means that the HTML documents themselves will be simpler and smaller. For these reasons the pages will download quicker.

A centralised repository for style, also means that you can make sure that all the pages for a given web site have a consistent style. This is of particular interest to corporations who may wish to maintain a corporate style for all their web pages.

In the new CSS2 standard there are many more recommendations that have started to be implemented. In particular they make many recommendations with the intention that web sites become accessible to all, and that all web sites should use style sheets. This includes people with various disabilities. Many of these recommendations have been incorporated in law. In this country there is the **disability discrimination act**.

One form of discrimination is to produce web sites that are not accessible to sections of the population. Web designers need to be aware that people may not have the latest computer or browser. Also, that people who are visually impaired may not be able to read text. In the past some attempt to alleviate this was to carefully choose the colours and size of text. Nowadays technology has provided us with aural style sheets that can be used in conjunction with special-purpose browsers with a built-in speech synthesiser. An example of which can be downloaded from the Internet - called Simply Web 2000.

Exercise 11-2

1. Explain what is meant by a style sheet, and describe how it can be used by a set of web pages.

2. Describe the advantages of including cascading style sheets on a corporate web site. Include the expressions: less code, easy maintenance, consistent style, faster download of pages.

3. Create an HTML file that contains the heading "personal statement". This should be a size 2 heading. Then add 3 paragraphs about yourself. Save this file as personalinfo.html.

4. Create an external style sheet called style1.css to specify the font-type and colour of text for the heading.

5. Add style rules for the paragraphs so that when you start a new paragraph it is indented by 0.5cm. Also choose the font-size and font-type.

6. Modify personalinfo.html so that it links to the style sheet style1.css. Check out how the html file appears with this style sheet.

7. Explain what is meant by the CSS box model. Describe how it can be employed to create padding, borders, and margins etc.

8. Create another style sheet. Call it style2.css. Within this style sheet create a rule for creating a red background for the heading. Add rules to provide top and bottom margins of 0.75cm, and left and right margins of 1cm.

9. Test out style sheet style2.css by modifying personalinfo.html so that it links to style2.css instead.

10. Write another web page, this time called education.html. In it include a size 2 heading called "Education" and 3 or 4 paragraphs that talk about what you studied in the last few educational establishments that you last studied at. Include an embedded style sheet within the head of the document. This should include style statements that specify the colour and font-type of size 2 headings. Load this web page to demonstrate the cascade effect of style sheets.

Chapter 12 (week 12)

Tables

12.1 A first table

The following shows how a table can be used to tabulate data.

<u>Example 41</u>

```
<html>
<table>
     <tr> <td> Colmerauer, A <td> 92 <td> 37 <td> 65
     <tr> <td> Hopper, G <td> 73 <td> 56 <td> 45
     <tr> <td> Kemeny, J <td> 78 <td> 67 <td> 76
     <tr> <td> Kernighan, B <td> 56 <td> 59 <td> 83
     <tr> <td> Ritchie, D <td> 60 <td> 78 <td> 89
     <tr> <td> Stroustrup, B <td> 49 <td> 64 <td> 76
     <tr> <td> Wirth, N <td> 87 <td> 74 <td> 82
</table>
</html>
```

Notes:

1. The contents of a table are defined between the tags <TABLE> and </TABLE>.

2. The tag <tr> used to specify a new row in the table.

3. The tag <td> denotes table data. Each time you want to put an item of data in a row, you need to precede it with the tag <td>.

4. You will notice that the width of the column is determined by the width of the data.

12.2   Use of headers and colspan

The following is based on the previous table. This time we have added table headers and introduced the use of colspan.

Example 42

```
<html
<head><title>Use of tables 1</title></head>
<body>
<table>
     <tr align = "center"> <th colspan = "4"> Student marks
     <tr align = "left"> <th> Name <th> Maths <th> English <th>
                              Science
     <tr> <td> Colmerauer, A <td> 92 <td> 37 <td> 65
     <tr> <td> Hopper, G <td> 73 <td> 56 <td> 45
     <tr> <td> Kemeny, J <td> 78 <td> 67 <td> 76
     <tr> <td> Kernighan, B <td> 56 <td> 59 <td> 83
     <tr> <td> Ritchie, D <td> 60 <td> 78 <td> 89
     <tr> <td> Stroustrup, B <td> 49 <td> 64 <td> 76
     <tr> <td> Wirth, N <td> 87 <td> 74 <td> 82
</table>
</body></html>
```

Notes:

1. Alignment can be "left" , "right" , or "center".

2. Colspan specifies how many columns in each row. This is needed because the first row contains one data item, and this spans 4 rows.

3. The tag <th> denotes a table heading. It is normal to have a table heading in each table so that a user knows what the data refers to.

4. In this example there are 2 rows of table headings. The first is general and spans all the columns of the tables. The second row describes the data in each column.

5. You will notice that some of the columns are wider to allow for the headings to fit in.

A table with headings and using column span

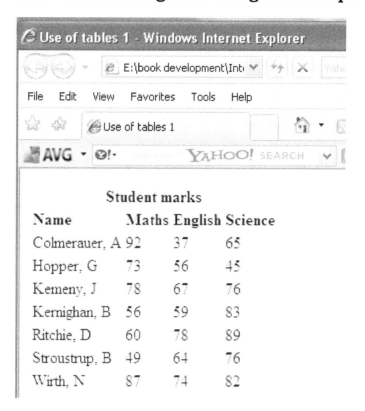

12.3   Cell padding and cell spacing

<u>Example 43</u>

```
<html
<head><title>Use of tables 2</title></head>
<body>
<table border = 1 cellpadding = 10 callspacing = 5 >
     <tr align = "center"> <th colspan = "4"> Student marks
     <tr align = "left"> <th> Name <th> Maths <th> English  <th>
                         Science
     <tr> <td> Colmerauer, A <td> 92 <td> 37 <td> 65
     <tr> <td> Hopper, G <td> 73 <td> 56 <td> 45
     <tr> <td> Kemeny, J <td> 78 <td> 67 <td> 76
     <tr> <td> Kernighan, B <td> 56 <td> 59 <td> 83
     <tr> <td> Ritchie, D <td> 60 <td> 78 <td> 89
     <tr> <td> Stroustrup, B <td> 49 <td> 64 <td> 76
     <tr> <td> Wirth, N <td> 87 <td> 74 <td> 82
</table>
</body></html>
```

Notes:

1. Width and height can be used to specify a table size. Without these attributes the size of the table is determined by the data.

2. The attribute **cellpadding** determines the amount of space around the data in each cell of the table.

3. The **border** attribute determines the size of the border around each cell of the table. If border is set to 0, then there will be no visible border.

4. The **cellspacing** attribute sets the amount of space between table borders.

Table with cell padding and cell spacing

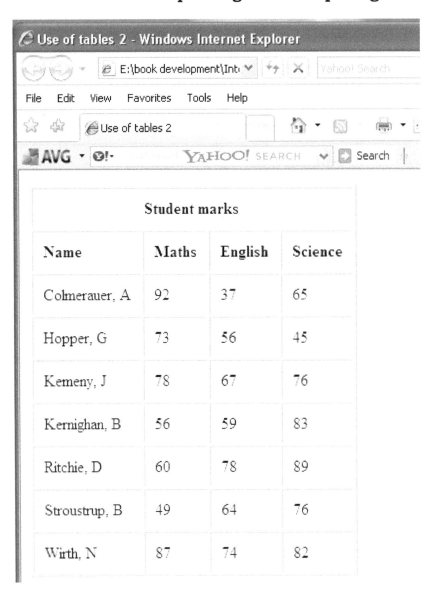

12.4   Table and Cell content alignment

In this example we start with the first table in this chapter and consider how that table can be centred. I have the centred the first data item for each row.

Example 44

```
<html>
<center>
<table>
    <tr> <td align = center> Colmerauer, A <td>92<td>37<td>65
    <tr> <td align = center> Hopper, G <td> 73 <td> 56 <td> 45
    <tr> <td align = center> Kemeny, J <td> 78 <td> 67 <td> 76
    <tr> <td align = center> Kernighan, B <td> 56 <td> 59 <td>83
    <tr> <td align = center> Ritchie, D <td>60 <td>78 <td> 89
    <tr> <td align = center> Stroustrup, B <td>49 <td>64 <td>76
    <tr> <td align = center> Wirth, N <td> 87 <td> 74 <td> 82
</table>
</html>
```

Notes:

1. The <center> tag immediately above <table> is used to centre everything that follows.

2. Each data item can be aligned. In this case align = center. You can however have left or right alignment if you choose.

181

12.5   Column width

The problem with the previous example is that the numbers are all squashed together. You could avoid this problem by setting the width for each column. You can size the width of the table itself as a percentage of the width of the page, as well as specifying the width of each column.

Example 45

```
<html>
<table width = 100%>
        <tr> <td width = 55%> Colmerauer, A <td width = 15%> 92
            <td width = 15%> 37 <td width = 15%> 65
        <tr> <td> Hopper, G <td> 73 <td> 56 <td> 45
        <tr> <td> Kemeny, J <td> 78 <td> 67 <td> 76
        <tr> <td> Kernighan, B <td> 56 <td> 59 <td> 83
        <tr> <td> Ritchie, D <td> 60 <td> 78 <td> 89
        <tr> <td> Stroustrup, B <td> 49 <td> 64 <td> 76
        <tr> <td> Wirth, N <td> 87 <td> 74 <td> 82
</table>
</html>
```

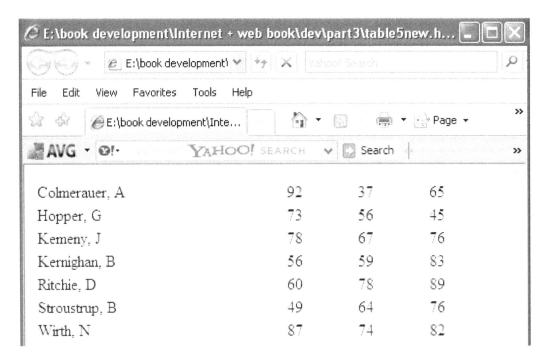

Notes:

1. You only need to set the width for each data item for 1 row. These percentages widths given to each item of data represents a percentage of the width of the table.

2. If you change the width for the table, the corresponding column widths will change also.

12.6 Pictures and background colour of table cells

<u>Example 46</u>

```
<html>
<head><title>Use of tables 3</title></head>
<body>
<table border = 1 cellpadding = 10 cellspacing = 5>
    <tr align = "center"> <th colspan = "3" bgcolor =#FFB080>
        Apparatus used in Chemistry
    <tr> <th bgcolor = #B0ff80> Name
         <th bgcolor = #80B0FF> Picture
         <th bgcolor = #ff80B0> description
    <tr> <td> Beaker
         <td><img src = "beaker.jpg" height = 100 width = 100>
         <td> Beaker is used for mixing chemicals
    <tr> <td> Conical flask
         <td> <img src = "conical_flask.jpg">
         <td> Useful for titrations
    <tr> <td> Volumetric flask
         <td> <img src = "volumetric_flask.jpg"
                 height = 100 width = 100>
         <td> Used to make solutions of known concentration.
</table>
</body></html>
```

Notes:

1. The **bgcolor** attribute is used to set the background colour of a table cell in the same manner that you would with the body of a web page.

2. In this example the first row that spans 3 columns is coloured light orange.

3. The cells in the next row are coloured green, blue and pink

4. Pictures can be considered to be table data. An image can be inserted using the <IMG> tag as before.

5. If the pictures are too large, you can adjust the size using the height and width attributes.

Table with background colour and pictures

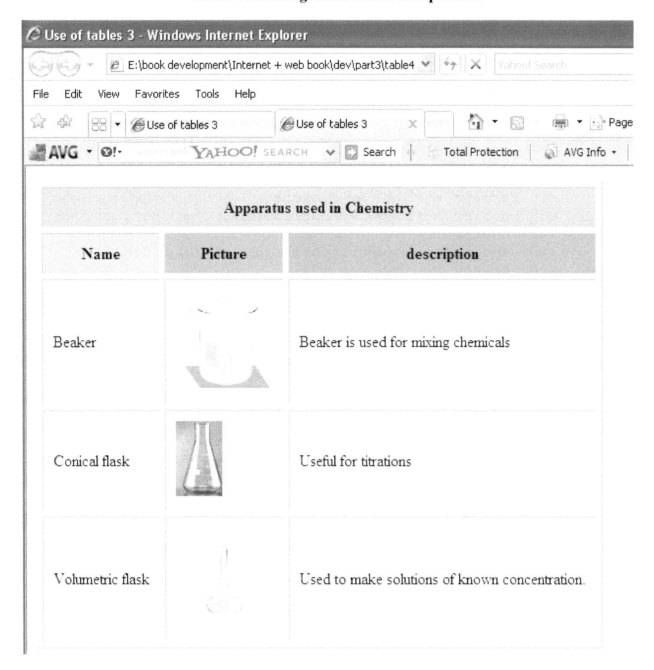

Apparatus used in Chemistry		
Name	**Picture**	**description**
Beaker		Beaker is used for mixing chemicals
Conical flask		Useful for titrations
Volumetric flask		Used to make solutions of known concentration.

12.7   Vertical alignment

You can align text vertically in as table cell as well as horizontally. This example adds to the previous example. In this case we have used the **valign** attribute to align the text for the third column of each row.

Example 47

```
<html>
<head><title>Use of tables 3</title></head>
<body>
<table border = 1 cellpadding = 10 cellspacing = 5>
     <tr align = "center"> <th colspan = "3" bgcolor =#FFB080>
        Apparatus used in Chemistry
     <tr>  <th bgcolor = #BOff80> Name
           <th bgcolor = #80BOFF> Picture
           <th bgcolor = #ff80BO> description
     <tr> <td> Beaker
          <td><img src = "beaker.jpg" height = 100 width = 100>
          <td valign = top> Beaker is used for mixing chemicals
     <tr> <td> Conical flask
          <td> <img src = "conical_flask.jpg">
          <td valign = middle> Useful for titrations
     <tr> <td> Volumetric flask
          <td> <img src = "volumetric_flask.jpg"
                  height = 100 width = 100>
          <td valign = bottom> Used to make solutions of known concentration.
</table>
</body></html>
```

Notes:

1. The align attribute when added to the <td> tag, is used to align the text horizontally. The possible values are left, center, and right.

2. The valign attribute when added to the <td> tag, is used to align the text vertically. The possible values are top, middle, and bottom.

3. This example uses all 3 values.

Table with text showing vertical alignment

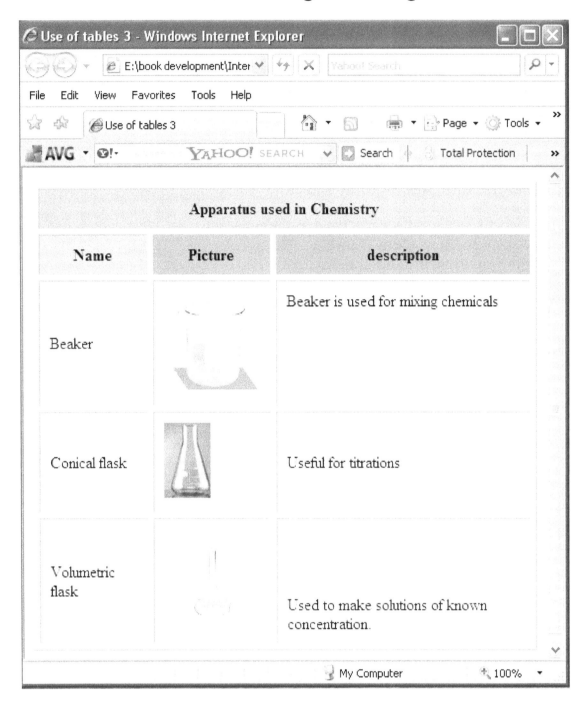

12.8   Use of rowspan

<u>Example 48</u>

```
<HTML>

<TABLE cellpadding = 5 cellspacing = 10 border = 4 bordercolor =
blue>

    <TR>
        <TD ROWSPAN = 3>Unit 6 <BR>Further HTML
        <TD>Style sheets
        <TD>27<sup>th</sup>March 2006
    <TR>
        <TD>Use of Tables
        <TD>17<sup>th</sup>April 2006
    <TR>
        <TD>Use of forms
        <TD>24<sup>th</sup>April 2006
</table>

</HTML>
```

Notes:

1.   ROWSPAN = 3 is used to indicate that one cell will take up 3 rows.

2.   BORDERCOLOR is used to indicate the colour of the border.

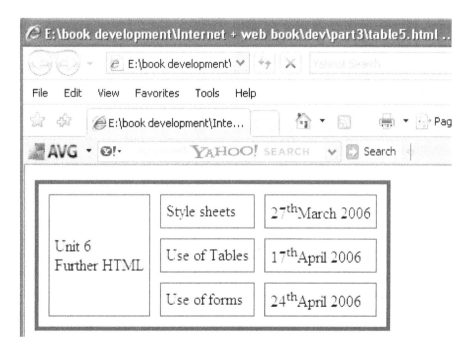

12.9   Nested tables

Example 49

```
<html>
<table border = 0 Cellspacing = 4 BGCOLOR = #cccccc>
   <caption><B>Computing Bibliography</B></caption>
   <TR>
     <TD>
        <Table border = 10 cellpadding = 4><caption>C++ books</caption>
           <tr><td>Hubbard, John
              <td>Programming with C++
           <tr><td>Oualline, Steve
              <td>Practical C++ programming
           <tr><td>Ammeraal, Leendert
              <td>C++ for programmers
           <tr><td>Stroustrup, Bjarne
              <td>The C++ programming language
        </table>
     </TD>
     <TD>
        <Table border = 10 cellpadding = 4><caption>HTML books</caption>
           <tr><td>Castro, Elizabeth
              <td>HTML for the World Wide Web
           <tr><td>Oliver, D & Holzschlag, M
              <td>Teach yourself HTML 4 in 24 hours
           <tr><td>Musciano, C & Kennedy, B
              <td>HTML The definitive guide
        </table>
     </TD>
   </TR>
</table>
</html>
```

Computing Bibliography

C++ books

Hubbard, John	Programming with C++
Oualline, Steve	Practical C++ programming
Ammeraal, Leendert	C++ for programmers
Stroustrup, Bjarne	The C++ programming language

HTML books

Castro, Elizabeth	HTML for the World Wide Web
Oliver, D & Holzschlag, M	Teach yourself HTML 4 in 24 hours
Musciano, C & Kennedy, B	HTML The definitive guide

Notes:

1.   One or more tables can be nested inside another table. In this case the table data is the entire contents of a table.

2. A caption is a heading or text associated with a table.

Exercise 12-1

1. Write HTML code to display the following table:

   1. Mathematics   496
   2. Physics   391
   3. Computing   287

Note: You may need to size the table cells to achieve this.

2. Write HTML code to produce a table as follows:

Section 1	25 marks
Section 2	10 marks
Section 3	15 marks

3. Demonstrate how a table can be used to help with layout of a picture and text. Create a simple table that consists of 1 row and two columns. Include a picture in the left column. In the right column include text to describe the picture Make sure that the image is properly sized so that each column is roughly the same size. Include cell padding so that the text isn't touching the picture.

4. Write HTML code to produce the following timetable. Experiment with different borders and cell spacing.

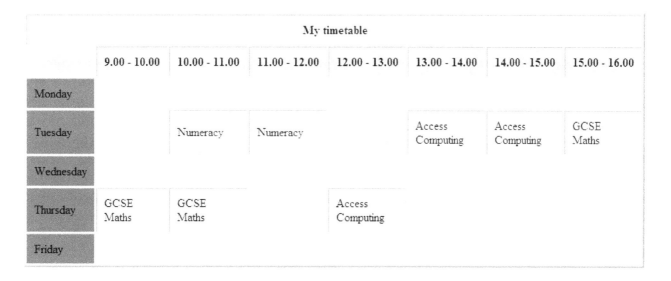

My timetable							
	9.00 - 10.00	10.00 - 11.00	11.00 - 12.00	12.00 - 13.00	13.00 - 14.00	14.00 - 15.00	15.00 - 16.00
Monday							
Tuesday		Numeracy	Numeracy		Access Computing	Access Computing	GCSE Maths
Wednesday							
Thursday	GCSE Maths	GCSE Maths		Access Computing			
Friday							

189

Chapter 13 (week 13)

Using forms

13.1   What is a form?

A form is part of a web page that collects information from users who visit that page. Users are able to enter information in a variety of ways, and this information is sent to a web server. The word server is often confused when talking about processing forms. Do we mean by this, the computer that is used for doing the processing, or the program responsible for managing the web pages – also called a server? Either way we will not concern ourselves here, as we won't be looking at this aspect of form processing.

When you create the layout of a form using HTML, there are a number of controls that you can use, to enter data in different ways. We will look at the following:

1. Text boxes – to enter a single line of text.
2. Textarea – to enter several lines of text.
3. Radio button – This facility allows you to choose 1 item from several choices. If you click on a different radio button, the previously chosen button becomes unchecked.
4. Check box – this looks like a radio button, except you can click on more than one item.
5. Drop-down menu – like the menus you have in your browser. Clicking on the menu option, brings down a drop-down menu. You can then choose 1 item by clicking on it.

Each of the controls that you include in your form needs to be given a name. This name serves as a label so that the particular item can be processed by the form-handler that is stored on the server. The form-handler is usually a CGI script.

A CGI (Common Gateway Interface) script is a program that interacts with your web page and the server. It is usually written in perl, but can in fact be written in other languages such as C++ or Visual Basic. Writing CGI scripts is beyond the scope of this course for two reasons. Firstly, it is another programming language that needs to be learnt – and this takes time. Secondly, you need to be allowed to run CGI programs on your computer to be able to use them. This requires a web server to be running on the computer you use. If you are using college computers, this requires the system manager to set this up for you. They may be reluctant to do this, as running CGI scripts poses a significant security problem.

Rather than use CGI scripts, we will be using the default email program. So that any data collected in the form will be emailed to someone.

13.2   A simple form

In the example that follows we will simply be sending someone some data collected using text boxes. Each text box collects a single line of data. We will not be considering how to process this data. We will simply send it to someone using email.

Example 50

```
<html>
<FORM METHOD = "POST" ACTION = "mailto:tony_hawken@talktalk.net"
enctype = "text/plain">

     Please enter your details<P>
     Name: <INPUT TYPE = "text" SIZE = "40" NAME = name> <P>
     tel: <INPUT TYPE = "text" SIZE = "15" NAME = tel> <P>

     <INPUT TYPE = "submit" VALUE = "submit">
     <INPUT TYPE = "Reset"  VALUE = "Reset">
</FORM>
</html>
```

Notes:

1. The METHOD attribute is used to indicate how the data is to be sent to the web server.

2. METHOD = "post" appends form data to the browser request. A program located on the web server can then access this data. As we are going to send the data to an email program, "post" will always be used.

3. The alternative is METHOD = "get". This option appends the form data directly to the end of the URL.

4. The attribute ACTION is used to specify which program is going to be used to process the data collected by the form. In this case the mailto protocol indicates that an email is to be sent. The text that follows mailto: is an email address where the data from the form will be sent.

5. **INPUT type = "text"** is used to specify that a text box is to be created. The SIZE attribute specifies the maximum number of characters that can fit in the text box.

6. **INPUT type = "submit"** creates a button that is used to submit the form. You use this button once you have completed the form. The action of submitting the form is to send the data to the specified form-handler. In this case an email.

7. **INPUT type = "reset"** creates a button that is used to clear the data from the form. You use this if you make a total mess of filling in the form and want to start again.

Email with form data

13.3   text boxes and text area boxes

In this example we have included the facility to enter multiple lines of text.

Example 51

```
<html>
<HR COLOR = "Blue" WIDTH = 100% HEIGHT = 2>

<H2>Project proposal</H2>
It is your job to choose what aspect of mathematics that you wish
to research and write about. For many this is a very daunting
task. For one thing it is very difficult to choose a topic that is
attainable in the time-frame allowed, that will also satisfy all
the criteria. For that reason it is a good idea to test out your
ideas before commiting too much time to the research.

<FORM METHOD = "POST" ACTION = "mailto:tony_hawken@talktalk.net"
enctype = "text/plain">

    Please enter your details<P>
    Name: <INPUT TYPE = "text" SIZE = "40" NAME = name> <P>
    tel: <INPUT TYPE = "text" SIZE = "15" NAME = tel> <P>
    email: <INPUT TYPE = "text" SIZE = "40" NAME = email>
    <P>
    Enter a brief description of your proposal here, and I will
    try and return constructive advice.
    <P>

    message: <TEXTAREA NAME = message ROWS = 10 COLS = 60>
            </TEXTAREA>
    <P>

    <INPUT TYPE = "submit" VALUE = "submit">
    <INPUT TYPE = "Reset"  VALUE = "Reset">
</FORM>
<html>
```

Notes:

1. There are 3 text boxes in this example, to store name, telephone number and email address.

2. A text area box is used to write a message. In this case there are 10 lines, each line being 60 characters.

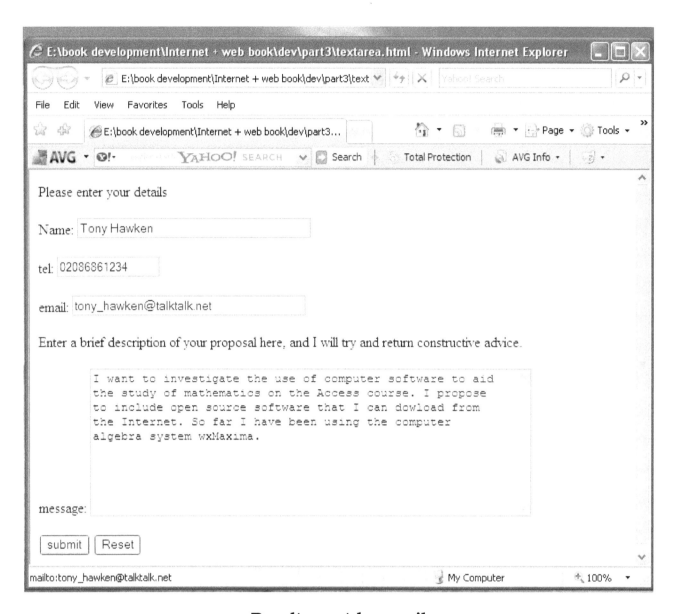

Results sent by email

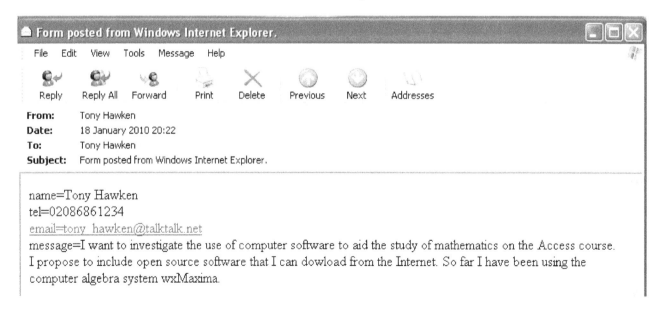

13.4 Radio buttons and check boxes

Example 52

```
<html>

<FORM METHOD = "POST" ACTION = "mailto:tony_hawken@talktalk.net"
enctype = "text/plain">

Please enter your details:
<P>
Name: <INPUT TYPE = "text" SIZE = "40" NAME = name> <P>

18-30 <INPUT type = "radio" NAME = age VALUE = 18-30 CHECKED>
31-40 <INPUT type = "radio" NAME = age VALUE = 31-40 >
41-50 <INPUT type = "radio" NAME = age VALUE = 41-50 >
51-60 <INPUT type = "radio" NAME = age VALUE = 51-60 >
61-70 <INPUT type = "radio" NAME = age VALUE = 61-70 >

<P>
Indicate previous programming experience:
<P>
BASIC<INPUT type = "checkbox" NAME = "programming" VALUE = "BASIC">
Pascal<INPUT type = "checkbox" NAME = "programming" VALUE = "Pascal">
C      <INPUT type = "checkbox" NAME = "programming" VALUE = "C">
C++   <INPUT type = "checkbox" NAME = "programming" VALUE = "C++"
        CHECKED>
Java  <INPUT type = "checkbox" NAME = "programming" VALUE = "Java">

<P>
      <INPUT TYPE = "submit" VALUE = "submit">
      <INPUT TYPE = "Reset"  VALUE = "Reset">

</FORM>
</html>
```

Notes:

1. A check box is similar in appearance to a radio button. However, with a radio button you can only store one value – the latest one you clicked on. But with a check box, you can have more than one value.

2. You can set a checked value for both check boxes and radio buttons. This is done using the CHECKED attribute. Remember that a radio button can only be checked once.

Form showing default values

Please enter your details:

Name: [   ]

18-30 ⊙ 31-40 ○ 41-50 ○ 51-60 ○ 61-70 ○

Indicate previous programming experience:

BASIC ☐ Pascal ☐ C ☐ C++ ☑ Java ☐

[submit] [Reset]

Form after filling in details

Please enter your details:

Name: [Tony Hawken   ]

18-30 ○ 31-40 ○ 41-50 ○ 51-60 ⊙ 61-70 ○

Indicate previous programming experience:

BASIC ☑ Pascal ☑ C ☑ C++ ☑ Java ☑

[submit] [Reset]

mailto:tony_hawken@talktalk.net

Email showing data collected

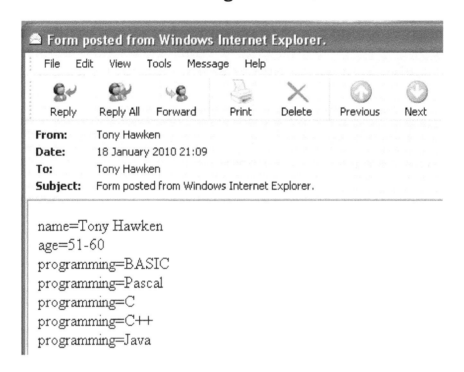

13.5 Select Menus

A pop-down menu is an ideal way to present a list of options to a user. They are very much like the pop-down menus that your are already familiar with, for example those available from the menu bar of Internet Explorer.

<u>Example 53</u>

```
<html>
Enter the year you were last in full education
<P>
<FORM METHOD = "POST" ACTION = "mailto:tony_hawken@talktalk.net"
enctype = "text/plain">

<P>Choose the year
<SELECT NAME = year SIZE = 3>
        <OPTION SELECTED> 2010
        <OPTION>    2009
        <OPTION>    2008
        <OPTION>    2007
        <OPTION>    2006
        <OPTION>    2005
        <OPTION>    2004
        <OPTION>    2003
        <OPTION>    2002
        <OPTION>    2001
</SELECT>

<P>
<INPUT TYPE = submit VALUE = "submit this">
<INPUT TYPE = reset VALUE = "Got it wrong!">
</FORM>

</BODY>
</HTML>
```

Notes:

1. The tag SELECT indicates that a menu is to follow. These menus are like those within your browser. In particular they have the property that you can scroll down the menu and you can select an option from the menu by clicking on it.

2. The attribute NAME is used to identify the menu. There may be more than one of these menus on a single form.

3. The tag SIZE is used to indicate the number of items that are visible within the menu at any one time. In this example 3 items will be displayed.

4. Each option in the menu is identified by the tag OPTION.

5. The attribute SELECTED indicates that the value associated with it is the default value. That is this value will be chosen unless the user changes it by clicking on another item in the menu.

Form when first loaded

email with form data

6. The default value for year is 2010. This is highlighted when the form is first loaded. I chose the year 2005, by scrolling down the menu and clicking on 2005. I then clicked on submit this and the data was emailed to myself.

13.6 Enter credit card details to make a donation

This is a more realistic looking example that uses a number of the form controls.

<u>Example 54</u>

```
<HTML>
<HEAD>    </HEAD>
<BODY>
<H1>Get me rich quick scheme</H1>

<FORM METHOD = "post" ACTION = "mailto:tony_hawken@talktalk.net">

Enter your full name
<INPUT TYPE = "Text" NAME = "PersonName" SIZE = 20>

<P>Click on the checkbox if you want to donate money to me.
<INPUT TYPE = checkbox Name = payme CHECKED>

<P>Enter your Credit card number
<INPUT TYPE = Text Name = CNum1 SIZE = 4>
<INPUT TYPE = Text Name = CNum2 SIZE = 4>
<INPUT TYPE = Text Name = CNum3 SIZE = 4>
<INPUT TYPE = Text Name = CNum4 SIZE = 4>

<P>Enter the expiration date
<INPUT TYPE = Text NAME = expdate SIZE = 6>

<P>Select your card type from the ones listed
<INPUT TYPE = radio NAME = payment VALUE = v CHECKED> Visa
<INPUT TYPE = radio NAME = payment VALUE = m > Mastercard
<INPUT TYPE = radio NAME = payment VALUE = o > Other

<P>Choose the size of donation
<SELECT NAME = amount SIZE = 3>
     <OPTION SELECTED> £10,000
     <OPTION>    £5,000
     <OPTION>    £1,000
     <OPTION>    £500
     <OPTION>    £100
     <OPTION>    £50
     <OPTION>    £10
</SELECT>

<P>Indicate why you want to donate money
<SELECT NAME = reason>
     <OPTION>You deserve it.
     <OPTION>I have more money than sense.
     <OPTION>I think you are a wonderful person.
```

```
        <OPTION>I want to pass my Computing Exam.
</SELECT>

<P>
<INPUT TYPE = submit VALUE = "submit this">
<INPUT TYPE = reset VALUE = "I've changed my mind">
</FORM>

</BODY>
</HTML>
```

What the form looks like:

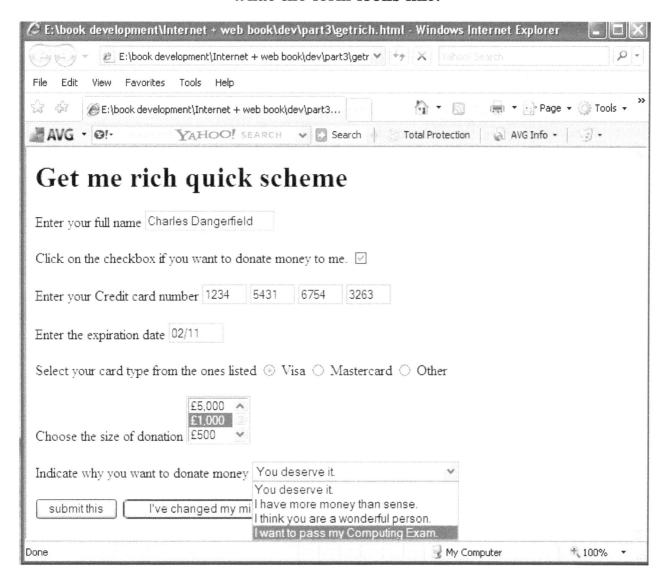

Notes:

1. This example demonstrates the use of a variety of types of input field.

2. A radio button is a collection of buttons, only one of which can be checked at any point in time. If you click on a different radio button, the previously checked one will become unchecked.

3. A check-box is similar to a radio button, except that more than one can be checked, or all of them can be unchecked. You can also easily spot a check box – it is square, whereas a radio button is circular.

4. A number of pop-down menus have been created.

5. Sometimes the data is sent as an attachment with file type .ATT. To view this you will have to go to the control panel and click on folder options. Then click on the tab file types. As this file type probably doesn't exist you will have to create a new file type. Click on new and type in ATT. Then choose a program to associate with this file type. I chose notepad. I also edited the output slightly, as the original output was all on one line and could not be displayed easily until I pressed return a few times to break up the line.

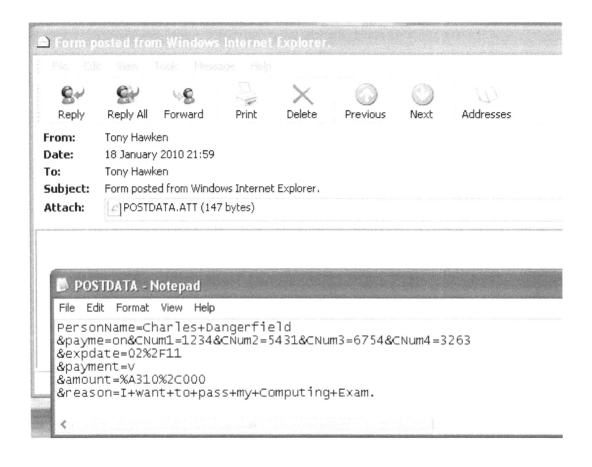

Exercise 13-1

1. Write a form that can be used to collect a name, address and telephone number. Let the form method be post, and for the ACTION specify your email address. Finally, Include a submit, and a reset button at the bottom of the form.

2. Write HTML code that creates a pop-up menu that looks like this

The mark I expect to get for this exam is:

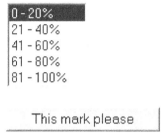

3. Create a web page that includes a form that can be used to carry out a simple Multiple-choice quiz. At the top of the form, there should be a space to enter a name. There should be at least 5 questions, and each question should have alternative answers. You should use radio buttons if there is only 1 possible correct answer. The results of an individual doing this quiz should be emailed to yourself.

Chapter 14 (week 14)

Further HTML Assignment

14.1   Assignment brief

Assignment for Unit 3

Further Web Site Development

You are required to produce a web-site containing at least 6 linked pages about one of the available optional subjects within the Access to Higher Education course. You would be best advised to choose one of the subjects that you are currently studying.

Task 1

1. Create a folder called unit3 for storing all files produced.

2. Within this folder create a shortcut that links to the notepad editor.

3. Produce a design that outlines the structure of a web-site containing a homepage and 6 subordinate pages. This design can be hand-written and should indicate how the pages are linked together.

4. Download suitable pictures that can be included in your web-site. If possible choose images that reflect the subject matter of the 6 units to be studied in the chosen subject.

Task 2

1. Write a few paragraphs describing the importance of style sheets on a corporate web site. You should include performance issues such as time taken to create web pages as well as time taken to download. Also talk about the **disability discrimination act**, and the possibility of using **aural style sheets**.

2. Create an HTML document called **homepage.html**. Include a heading and write at least 3 short paragraphs about the subject chosen. Include only the minimum of tags for formatting. You could for instance include such details as where and when lessons take place as well as the name of the teacher. Also include an anchor-point at the top of the page. Call this **Top**.

3. Include an embedded style sheet at the top of homepage.html. Use this style sheet to specify the formatting of paragraphs and font characteristics.

Task 3

1. Within homepage.html create a table containing 3 columns and 6 rows - one row for each unit. Use the first column to include the name of the unit. Use the second column to include a picture of your choice. And finally use the third column to include a link to the respective page containing information about the unit.

2. Modify your table so that a visible border is present.

3. Modify your table so that one or more cells in the table have a coloured background.

Task 4

Create an external style sheet called **mystyle.css** that includes the following features:

1. A tag to indicate how paragraphs are to be formatted. This should include a paragraph indent, and all paragraphs should be justified.

2. Tags to indicate the font characteristics. This should include size, colour and font-family used.

3. A tag to indicate the background colour, or background image to be used for each web page.

4. Tags to indicate the colour of links.

Task 5

Create a further 6 html documents - one for each unit. Call these documents **unit1.html** to **unit6.html** respectively.

1. Edit each of these documents in turn, so that each of them has a large heading and at least two paragraphs of text informing one about the nature of each unit.

2. For each of these documents include a link to the top part of the document **homepage.html**.

3. At the top of each of these documents add a link to the style sheet **mystyle.css**.

Task 6

1. Create an html document called question.html to be used to provide feedback about a course. This should include a form to provide feedback about a certain course. The results of this questionnaire should be emailed to your teacher.

2. The form should allow a user to enter their name on a single line. It should also allow them to enter their address on multiple lines.

3. Include a drop-down menu for a user to select their year of birth.

4. Then include a section that includes at least 6 questions, which can be answered using radio buttons.

5. Add a section that includes all the possible subjects available on the Access programme. This should have check-boxes to fill in, to indicate the subjects chosen.

6. Include both submit and reset buttons at the bottom of the form.

7. Add a table at the bottom that contains contact details for Croydon College. This table should have a coloured border.

Documentation required

1. A design as described in Task 1

2. A printout of the source code for each HTML document.

3. A printout of **homepage.html** and at least one of the other documents.

14.2   Task 1

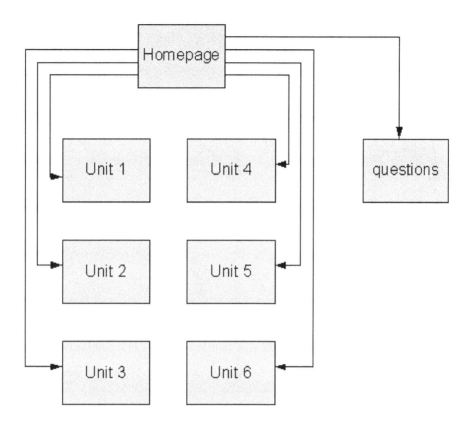

Notes

This diagram was completed using Open Office – Drawing. This is much easier to use than the basic drawing options in Microsoft Word, or in fact Microsoft Paint.

14.3   Task 2

q1   Importance of style sheets – see section 11.12

q2 + 3 follows:

<u>Example 55</u>

```
<HTML>
<HEAD> <title>Homepage for unit 3</title>

<style>
BODY      { margin-top: 0.25in;
          margin-left: 0.75in;
          margin-right: 0.75in}

H1    {font: 18pt Verdanna; color: #0000FF}

P     {font: 12pt Bookman; text-indent: 0.5in}
</style>
</HEAD>

<BODY background="blue_puzzle.jpg">
<A name = "Top">

<center><H1>Access Computing (2009 - 2010)</H1></center>


<P>
This course is intended for students who wish to follow a course
at university that has a significant element of computing -
particularly programming. It is also useful for courses such as
Physical Science courses and Engineering where some programming is
required.

<P>
It should not be confused with IT, where students learn how to use
application packages such as Microsoft WORD and Excel.

In the past successful students have gained places to study:
<UL>
      <LI>Computer Science and Mathematics - Queen Mary (University
          of London)
      <LI>Computer Science - City University (University of London)
      <LI>Computer Science - University of Westminster
      <LI>Business Information Systems - University of Westminster
      <LI>Computing - University of Kingston
      <LI>Business Information systems - University of Kingston
      <LI>Meteorology - University of Reading
</UL>
```

```
<P> The Access computing course has two main components -
    <OL>
            <LI>Programming using a 3GL (C++)
            <LI>The Internet and Web Design
    </OL>

The current programming language in use is the C++ programming
language. C++ is a hybrid language. That is you can carry out all
the things that can be done using C (Procedural paradigm), and in
addition to this you can write object-oriented programs. We will
be concentrating on the procedural parts of the language. Just
over half of the time is devoted to this. We will however be using
a modern C++ IDE (Quincy 2005), so our programs will have to
comply with the current ANSI standard.
<P>
The remainder of the course teaches how to access the internet,
and create web-pages using HTML. To do this, besides internet
access, you only require a web browser and a text editor such as
notepad.

</BODY>
</HTML>
```

Notes:

1. The embedded style sheet is really basic, but does satisfy the assessment criteria because it does deal with the style of paragraph and fonts. In addition the layout of the web page specifies the top, left and right margin sizes. Also the font, size, and colour of H1 headings are used. In this case the text colour is blue – but a different shade of blue to the background.

2. There are in all 4 paragraphs. Also, but not asked for, there is an unordered list. This uses skills previously taught. You shouldn't get penalized for adding things not asked for.

3. At the top there is an anchor point called "Top", as asked for.

Screen dump of web page

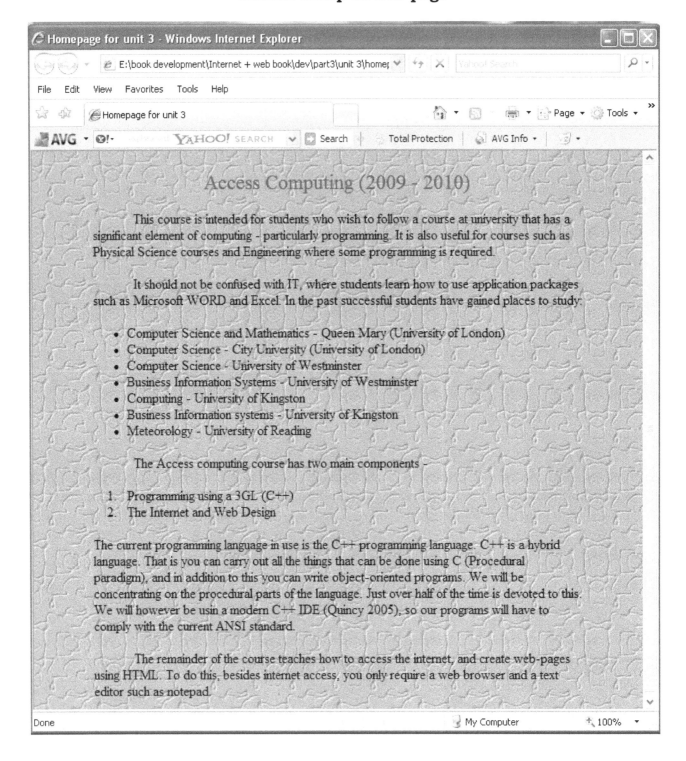

14.4   Task 3

This is a continuation of Task 2. You will notice that there is much that is the same in this code.

<u>Example 56</u>

```
<HTML>
<HEAD> <title>Homepage for unit 3</title>

<style>
BODY      { margin-top: 0.25in;
            margin-left: 0.75in;
            margin-right: 0.75in}

H1    {font: 18pt Verdanna; color: #0000FF}

P     {font: 12pt Bookman; text-indent: 0.5in}
</style>
</HEAD>

<BODY background="blue_puzzle.jpg">
<A name = "Top">

<center><H1>Access Computing (2009 - 2010)</H1></center>
<P>
This course is intended for students who wish to follow a course
at university that has a significant element of computing -
particularly programming. It is also useful for courses such as
Physical Science courses and Engineering where some programming is
required.
<P>
It should not be confused with IT, where students learn how to use
application packages such as Microsoft WORD and Excel. In the past
successful students have gained places to study:
<UL>
     <LI>Computer Science and Mathematics - Queen Mary (University
          of London)
     <LI>Computer Science - City University (University of London)
     <LI>Computer Science - University of Westminster
     <LI>Business Information Systems - University of Westminster
     <LI>Computing - University of Kingston
     <LI>Business Information systems - University of Kingston
     <LI>Meteorology - University of Reading
</UL>

<P> The Access computing course has two main components -
     <OL>
               <LI>Programming using a 3GL (C++)
               <LI>The Internet and Web Design
```

```
        </OL>


The current programming language in use is the C++ programming
language. C++ is a hybrid language. That is you can carry out all
the things that can be done using C (Procedural paradigm), and in
addition to this you can write object-oriented programs. We will
be concentrating on the procedural parts of the language. Just
over half of the time is devoted to this. We will however be using
a modern C++ IDE (Quincy 2005), so our programs will have to
comply with the current ANSI standard.
<P>


The remainder of the course teaches how to access the internet,
and create web-pages using HTML. To do this, besides internet
access,you only require a web browser and a text editor such as
notepad.
<P>
<table border = 1 cellpadding = 10 callspacing = 5>
     <tr align = "center"> <th colspan = "3"> Course Information
     <TR>
         <TH align = "center">Unit name
         <TH align = center>Picture
         <TH align = center>Link to unit page
     <TR><TD>Using the Internet and Email
         <TD><img src = "internetexplorer.jpg" height = 100 width
             = 100>
         <TD align = "center"><A href = "unit1.html">[Unit 1]</A>
     <TR><TD>Web development (HTML)
         <TD><img src = "html.jpg" height = 100 width = 100>
         <TD align = "center"><A href = "unit2.html">[Unit 2]</A>
     <TR><TD>Further web site development
         <TD><img src = "mywebpage.jpg" height = 100 width = 100>
         <TD align = "center"><A href = "unit3.html">[Unit 3]</A>
     <TR><TD>Basic programming skills in C++
         <TD><img src = "aboutquincy.jpg" height = 100 width =
             100>
         <TD align = "center"><A href = "unit4.html">[Unit 4]</A>
     <TR><TD>Further C++ programming
         <TD><img src = "BjarneStroustrup_pic_1.jpg" height = 100
             width = 100>
         <TD align = "center"><A href = "unit5.html">[Unit 5]</A>
     <TR><TD>Arrays, Structures and text file <BR>processing
         <TD><img src = "c++cover.jpg" height = 100 width = 100>
         <TD align = "center"><A href = "unit6.html">[Unit 6]</A>
</table>

</BODY>
</HTML>
```

Screen dump of part of web page showing a table

Course Information		
Unit name	**Picture**	**Link to unit page**
Using the Internet and Email		[Unit 1]
Web development (HTML)		[Unit 2]
Further web site development		[Unit 3]
Basic programming skills in C++		[Unit 4]
Further C++ programming		[Unit 5]
Arrays, Structures and text file		[Unit 6]

Done   My Computer   100%

14.5   Task 4

<u>Example 57</u>

```
<!-- Contents of mystyle.css   -->

BODY {background: lizardskin.gif; margin_top: 0.25in
      margin_left: 0.25in; margin_right: 0.25in   }

H1    {font: 14pt Verdanna; color blue    }

P     {font-family: Bookman; font-size: 12pt; text_align left;
       text_indent: 0.5in }

A:link    {color: blue}
A:active{color: red}
A:visited{color: green}
```

14.6   Task 5

Example 58

```
<HTML>
<HEAD>
     <TITLE>Unit 4</TITLE>
     <link rel = stylesheet href = "mystyle.css" type =
      "text/css">
</HEAD>
<BODY>

     <H3>Unit 1 </H3>
     <P>
     This unit introduces the C++ programming language.
     The unit includes the following topics:
     <P>
          Introduction to C++ programming,
          Create and run simple C++ programs using the Quincy 2005
          IDE, Declaring and using variables (different datatypes
          available), Simple input and output using <iostream>,
          Selection (if and switch statements), Simple program
          testing,
     <P>
     Go to top of homepage
     <A href = "homepage.html">[homepage]</A>

</BODY>
</HTML>
```

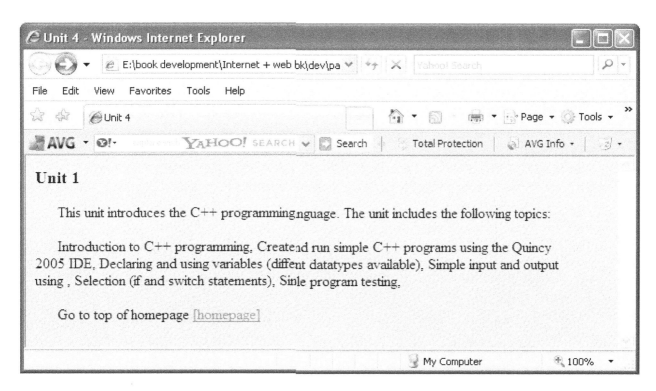

14.7   Task 6

<u>Example 59</u>

```
<html>
<head><title>question.html</title></head>

<body>
<H1> Course questionaire </H1>

<FORM METHOD = "POST" ACTION = "mailto:tony_hawken@talktalk.net"
enctype = "text/plain">

     Please enter your details<P>
     Name: <INPUT TYPE = "text" SIZE = "40" NAME = name> <P>
     address: <TEXTAREA Name = address rows = 4 COLS = 40>
     </TEXTAREA>
     <P>
     <P>Enter your year of birth<P>
     <SELECT NAME = year SIZE = 5>
          <OPTION SELECTED> 1990
          <OPTION>     1989
          <OPTION>     1988
          <OPTION>     1987
          <OPTION>     1986
          <OPTION>     1985
          <OPTION>     1984
          <OPTION>     1983
          <OPTION>     1982
          <OPTION>     1981
     </SELECT>
     <P>
     <H3>Questions about the course</H3>
     Click on the most appropriate answer
     <P>
     1. The teacher was confident and knew the subject <BR>
     Strongly agree<INPUT type = "radio" NAME = q1 VALUE = SA
     CHECKED>
     Agree<INPUT type = "radio" NAME = q1 VALUE = A>
     Neither agree or disagree
          <INPUT type = "radio" NAME = q1 VALUE = N>
     Disagree<INPUT type = "radio" NAME = q1 VALUE = D >
     Strongly disagree
          <INPUT type = "radio" NAME = q1 VALUE = SD>
     <P>
     2. The pace of the lesson was too fast <BR>
     Strongly agree<INPUT type = "radio" NAME = q2 VALUE = SA
     CHECKED>
     Agree<INPUT type = "radio" NAME = q2 VALUE = A>
     Neither agree or disagree
```

```
    <INPUT type = "radio" NAME = q2 VALUE = N>
Disagree<INPUT type = "radio" NAME = q2 VALUE = D >
Strongly disagree<INPUT type = "radio" NAME = q2 VALUE = SD>
<P>
3. The pace of the lesson was too slow <BR>
Strongly agree<INPUT type = "radio" NAME = q3 VALUE = SA
CHECKED>
Agree<INPUT type = "radio" NAME = q3 VALUE = A>
Neither agree or disagree
    <INPUT type = "radio" NAME = q3 VALUE = N>
Disagree<INPUT type = "radio" NAME = q3 VALUE = D >
Strongly disagree<INPUT type = "radio" NAME = q3 VALUE = SD>
<P>
4. The pace of the lesson was just right <BR>
Strongly agree<INPUT type = "radio" NAME = q4 VALUE = SA
CHECKED>
Agree<INPUT type = "radio" NAME = q4 VALUE = A>
Neither agree or disagree
    <INPUT type = "radio" NAME = q4 VALUE = N>
Disagree<INPUT type = "radio" NAME = q4 VALUE = D >
Strongly disagree<INPUT type = "radio" NAME = q4 VALUE = SD>
<P>
5. Comprehensive handouts were provided<BR>
Strongly agree<INPUT type = "radio" NAME = q5 VALUE = SA
CHECKED>
Agree<INPUT type = "radio" NAME = q5 VALUE = A>
Neither agree or disagree
    <INPUT type = "radio" NAME = q5 VALUE = N>
Disagree<INPUT type = "radio" NAME = q5 VALUE = D >
Strongly disagree<INPUT type = "radio" NAME = q5 VALUE = SD>
<P>
6. The teacher was always willing to answer questions<BR>
Strongly agree<INPUT type = "radio" NAME = q6 VALUE = SA
CHECKED>
Agree<INPUT type = "radio" NAME = q6 VALUE = A>
Neither agree or disagree
    <INPUT type = "radio" NAME = q6 VALUE = N>
Disagree<INPUT type = "radio" NAME = q6 VALUE = D >
Strongly disagree<INPUT type = "radio" NAME = q6 VALUE = SD>
<P>
<H3>Subjects taken this year</H3>
Communication <INPUT type = "checkbox" NAME = "subject" VALUE
 = "Communication" CHECKED>
Numeracy  <INPUT type = "checkbox" NAME = "subject" VALUE =
    "Numeracy" CHECKED>
IT <INPUT type = "checkbox" NAME = "subject" VALUE = "IT"
CHECKED>
<BR>
Mathematics L3 <INPUT type = "checkbox" NAME = "subject"
VALUE = "Mathematics L3">
Computing <INPUT type = "checkbox" NAME = "subject" VALUE =
```

```
        "Computing">
    Physics <INPUT type = "checkbox" NAME = "subject" VALUE =
        "Physics">
    <BR>
    Biology <INPUT type = "checkbox" NAME = "subject" VALUE =
        "Biology">
    Business studies<INPUT type = "checkbox" NAME = "subject"
    VALUE = "Business studies">
    English Lit <INPUT type = "checkbox" NAME = "subject" VALUE =
        "English Lit">
    <P>
    <H3>Contact details</H3>

    <TABLE cellpadding = 5 cellspacing = 10 border = 4
        bordercolor = blue>
    <TR>
        <TD>Address
        <TD>Croydon college, <BR>College Road,<BR> Croydon
    <TR>
        <TD>Web
        <TD>www.croydon.ac.uk
    <TR>
        <TD>telephone
        <TD>0208 686 5700
    </table>
    <P>

    <INPUT TYPE = "submit" VALUE = "submit">
    <INPUT TYPE = "Reset"  VALUE = "Reset">
</FORM>

</body>
<html>
```

Screen dump (first part of screen)

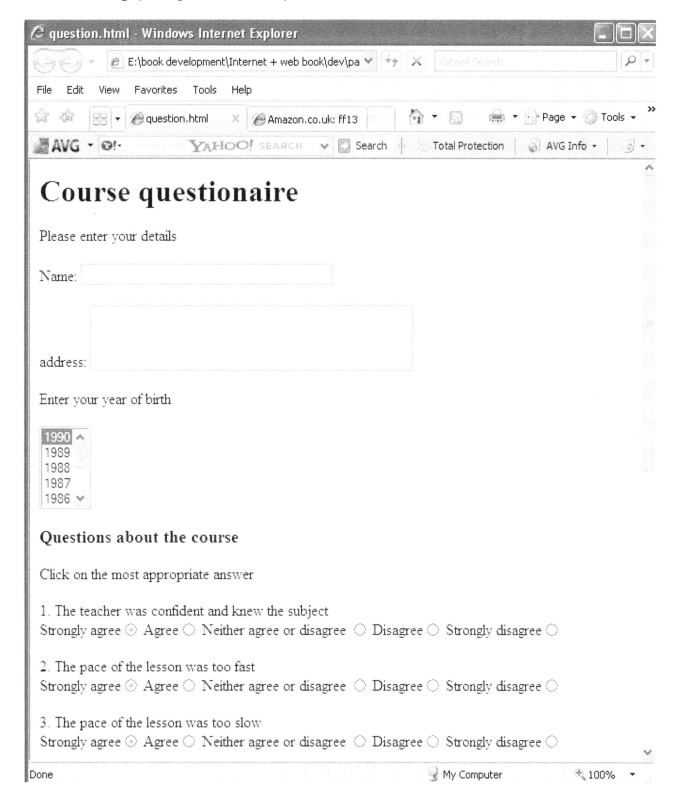

Screen dump (second part of screen)

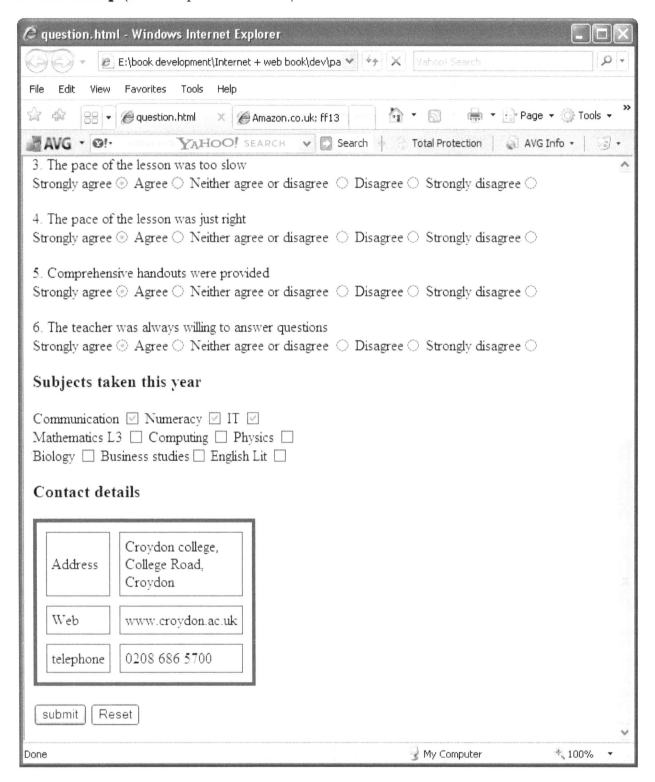

Notes

1. The 6 questions have been checked for Strongly agree. If the user does not click on radio button this option will be chosen
2. The check boxes for communication, numeracy and IT have been checked as these are core subjects.

Chapter 15(week 15)

Summary

15.1   Tasks to do

1. There is an element of research required for this unit. In particular you need to demonstrate that you understand the importance of style sheets for a corporate web site. This information can be found in many books and also on the web. You need to be looking at the advantages of style sheets. You should also be emphasizing the fact that all web sites should be using them. See section 11.12.

2. The previous example assignment also asks you to do research on the disability discrimination act and how web sites are affected by this. It also asks you to look into aural style sheets. There is much material on the Internet about these topics. If you have time you may even consider downloading software to try out. In any case, even if you are not asked to do this in your assignment specification, it is a really good example to get you thinking about issues of accessibility.

3. The assignment for this unit requires you to think about design. You don't have to do much, but you will have to think in advance about how you want the web pages to look . You will need to sketch one or more web pages to show how you would like them to appear. Also, you need to think about how the various web pages will link together. This is often dictated by how you think a user will move from one page to the next by following links. To represent how the web pages link together, a structure chart will have to be drawn. For best results use the drawing tool within OpenOffice.

4. Once you know what common style you want for a number of web pages, it is time to create a style sheet to specify this style. You are only expected to create very simple style sheets for this assignment. It helps if you have something to test it on, so you really needed to have created at least one HTML document that links to this style sheet. You can then modify the style sheet incrementally, and then test it out with a given HTML file continuously by clicking on the refresh button after each set of changes that you have made to the style sheet.

5. Tables are relatively easy to produce, even relatively complicate ones if you create them incrementally. You can always create an outline table that has the right number of rows and columns. You can then add features such as cell padding or borders at a later date. Remember inserting a picture into a table is as easy as adding text. After the tag <TD> you just need to add the code necessary for adding a picture.

6. The form required for this assignment contains many elements. These too can be added incrementally. The overall structure and code to represent the different components can be worked out by looking at the examples in this book.

7. Once you have a web site that is as asked for, you will need to supply documentation to demonstrate this. The source code for each web page or style sheet can be copied and pasted into a word-processed document. How the web pages appear can be demonstrated by obtaining a screen dump.

15.2   Unit summary

1. A web design can be represented by a storyboard. This is made up of a site plan (that looks like a structure chart) to indicate how the different web pages are linked and also a sketch of each web page indicating the layout.

2. An external style sheet specifies a style for one or more html documents.

3. This simplifies the HTML for each web page as a style is specified for each tag, meaning that you do not have to add any attributes for the tags which have had a style specified for them.

4. It also means that all of the web pages that link to a given style sheet will have a uniform style or appearance.

5. If you include an embedded style sheet within an HTML document, this style sheet will override the external style sheet. We say that there has been a cascade, hence cascading style sheets (CSS).

6. The CSS box model indicates how you can add margins, padding and borders to a variety of elements. These elements include paragraphs and headings. As well as this you can specify the size of the content. Here content refers to the paragraph or heading etc which is having a style applied to it.

7. A table is specified between the tags <TABLE> and </TABLE>

8. Each table is made up of a number of rows which start with the tag <TR>

9. Within each row you have one or more columns which are created each time you enter some table data. Each item of table data starts with the tag <TD>

10.   You can include data in a number of different formats. It could be simple text, text with other HTML tags, a picture, or indeed another table (A nested table).

11.   You can apply a border to a table as well as including cell spacing and cell padding. Also, within a given row, or even individual data items within a row, you can specify how text or images will be aligned.

12. You can make a table element span a number or columns in a table using the <colspan> tag.

13. You can make a table element span a number of rows within a table using the <rowspan> tag.

14. A table is a good way to arrange both text and pictures.

15. You can make a web page more interactive by including a form.

16. A form allows you to collect data from a user.

17. This could mean using a simple text box, that allows you to collect a single line of data.

18. If you want more than one line, say for an address, you would create a text area.

19. You can click on a checkbox or radio button to indicate a choice. The difference between the two is that if you use a radio button, you can only ever have one choice. Clicking on a different radio button will delete a previous choice. Whereas, you can click on more than one check box if you like.

20. You can select a choice from a pop-down menu. These work just like the ones you have on your browser.

21. In each case you need to specify an action when the form has been completed. The action is normally involves running a CGI script. In this book we have only used the default mail program to send the data by email.

22. You indicate that a form has been completed by clicking on a SUBMIT button. If you make a mess of things you can clear the form by clicking on a REST button.

Bibliography

General Computing

1. Norton, Peter. Computing fundamentals 6/e. McGraw-Hill 2006

The Internet and Email

2. Berners-Lee, Tim. Weaving the Web: The Past, Present and Future of the World Wide Web by the Inventor 1/e. Orion Business 1999

3. Buchanan, William. Mastering the Internet. Macmillan 1997

4. Calishain, Tara & Dornfest, Rael. Google hacks 2/e. O'Reilly 2004

5. Dietel, H.M & Dietel, P.J & Nieto, T.R. Internet & World Wide Web: How to program 2/e. Prentice-Hall 2002

6. Greenlaw, Raymond & Hepp, Ellen. In-line/On-line: Foundations of the Internet and the world wide web. McGraw-Hill 1999.

7. Lojkine, Mary. Internet in easy steps. Computer step 2003

8. Poremsky, Diane. Google and other search engines. Peachpit 2004

9. Quercia, Valerie. Internet in a nutshell. O'Reilly 1997

10. Schneider, Gary P. & Evans, Jessica. New perspectives on the Internet 6/e. Course Technology 2007.

11. Schneider, Gary P. & Evans, Jessica & Pinard, Katherine T. The Internet illustrated (introductory)4/e. Course Technology 2006

12. Snell, Ned. Teach yourself the Internet in 24 hours 6/e. Sams 2002

Web sites, HTML and CSS

13. Andrew, Rachel & Ullman, Chris & Waters, Crystal. Fundamental web design and Development Skills. Glasshaus 2002

14. Bordash, Michael et al. The Web Professional's Handbook. Glasshaus 2003

15. Castro, Elizabeth. HTML 4 for the World Wide Web 4/e. Peachpit press 2000

16. Castro, Elizabeth. HTML for the World Wide Web with XHTML and CSS 5/e, Peachpit press 2003

17. Ehlen, Anamary (ed). HTML complete 2/e. Sybex 2000

18. Hayes, Deidre. Teach yourself HTML 4 in 10 minutes 2/e. Sams 1999

19. Lemay, Laura. Teach yourself Web Publishing with HTML and XHTML in 21 days 3/e. Sams 2001

20. Lemay, Laura. Teach yourself Web Publishing with HTML 4 in a week 4/e. Sams 1997

21. Lojkine, Mary. Web graphics in easy steps. Computer Step 2003

22. McDonald, Mathew. Creating Web sites: The missing manual 1/e. Pogue press / O'Reilly 2006

23. McGrath, Mike. HTML in easy steps 5/e. Computer step 2006

24. Oliver, Dick & Holzschlag, Molly. Teach yourself HTML 4 in 24 hours. Sams 1997

25. Vandome, Nick. Creating Web Pages. Computer Step 2004

26. Wang, Paul S. & Katila, Sandra. An Introduction to Web Design and Programming. Brooks Cole 2004

27. Weakley, Russ. Teach yourself CSS in 10 minutes. Sams 2006

Resources on the Internet

World Wide Web Consortium

World Wide Web Consortium (w3c)
http://www.w3.org/

W3C Markup Validation Service (HTML, XHTML, SML and MathML)
http://validator.w3.org/

W3C CSS Validation Service
http://jigsaw.w3.org/CSS-Validation

History of the Web

A little history of the World Wide Web
http://www.w3.org/History.html

WorldWideWeb (Wikipedia)
http://en.wikipedia.org/wiki/WorldWideWeb

The World Wide Web (WWW) – William Stuart
http://www.livinginternet.com/w/w.htm

HTML and CSS

HTML tutorial (W3schools)
http://www.w3schools.com/html

HTML and CSS tutorials and stuff
http://htmldog.com/

HTML codes tutorial
http://www.htmlcodetutorial.com/

Index

U

U tag 97
UL tag 109-110
Underline 97
Uniform Resource Locator 9
unix 2
Unordered list 109-110
URL 9

V

Valign attribute 185

W

W3C 85,156,22
Web browser 7,57-58
Webmail 80
Width attribute 105-106
WINRAR 47
Wireframe 154
World Wide Web (WWW)
2,81,84-86

Z

ZIP format 47-48
ZIPCentral 47-48

www.ingramcontent.com/pod-product-compliance
Lightning Source LLC
Chambersburg PA
CBHW081226050326
40689CB00016B/3691